Homeschooling More Than One Child

Homeschooling More Than One Child

A Practical Guide for Families

Carren W. Joye

iUniverse, Inc.
New York Lincoln Shanghai

Homeschooling More Than One Child
A Practical Guide for Families

iUniverse books may be ordered through booksellers or by contacting:

iUniverse
2021 Pine Lake Road, Suite 100
Lincoln, NE 68512
www.iuniverse.com
1-800-Authors (1-800-288-4677)

ISBN: 0-595-34259-0

Printed in the United States of America

To my mom, who modeled for me through words and actions
that education is important, not school

To my husband, who knew before I did that home education
is the best option for our four children

Contents

Acknowledgments xi

Introduction xiii
    Who This Book Is For xiv
    How To Use This Book xv

Chapter 1   Getting Started: Jumping In With Both Feet 1
    Five Steps to Getting Started 2
    Transitioning to Homeschooling 4

Chapter 2   For the Record: Organizing the Paperwork 6
    Reasons for Keeping Records 7
    Record-keeping Methods 7
    Organizing Records for Multiple Students 10

Chapter 3   The Right Curriculum To Suit Each Child 11
    Teaching Methods and Styles 12
    Family Issues to Consider 14
    Purchasing a Curriculum for Multiple Ages 15
    Finding the Right Curriculum 16
    Supplementing Your Curriculum 17
    Teaching Required Subjects 18
    Designing Your Own Curriculum 20
    Knowing What to Teach 21
    Testing 22
    Relaxed Homeschooling 22

Chapter 4   The Penny-Pinching Homeschooler:
                      Affording Materials on One Income 24
    Usability of Packaged Curricula 25
    Tips for a Customized Curriculum 25
    How To Stay on a Budget 26
    Resources for Free and Inexpensive Materials 27
    Using Open Source Software 29
    Creative Ways to Pay for Supplies 30
    Ways To Cut Expenses 31

Chapter 5   **Storage and Supplies: What You Need and**
                  What You Can Get by Without 33
Supply Checklists 34
Storing Supplies 35
Storing Books 35
Displaying and Storing Artwork and Projects 36
The Work Area 37
Files and Notebooks 38
Containers 39
Color-Coding 39
Home Computer 39

Chapter 6   **Secrets of the One-Room Schoolhouse** 41
Sharing Subjects 42
The Option to Skip Grades 43
Keeping Their Attention 44
Scheduling One-on-One Instruction 45
Independent Study 45
Keeping Each Child Focused 46
Managing Interruptions 47
How Older Children Can Help 48
How Family and Friends Can Help 48
Handling Multiple Learning Styles 49

Chapter 7   **Plans and Schedules: Making the**
                  Most of Your Time 51
Advance Preparation 51
Sample Yearly Schedules 52
Planning Your Own Yearly Schedule 53
Sample Weekly and Daily Schedules 54
Scheduling Your Week 55
Scheduling Your Day 55
Schedules and To-Do Lists for Students 56
Multi-tasking 57
Making the Schedule Work 57
Homeschooling Through an Illness or Crisis 59

Chapter 8   **Homeschooling with Little Ones Underfoot** 61
Nap Time and Quiet Time 62
Toddler-proof Your House 62
Including Little Ones During School Time 63

"School Time Only" Box 63
Educational Games and Programs 64
Getting Help from Others 64
Change Your Homeschooling Methods 65

Chapter 9   If You Have Elementary and Middle Schoolers 67
Preparing a Learning Environment 67
How To Avoid Busy Work 68
Keeping Children Focused 69
Talking and Reading to Children 70
The Importance of Playtime 70

Chapter 10   Handling Junior High and High Schoolers 72
High School Requirements 73
Handling Difficult Subjects 74
College Preparation 75
Alternatives to College 77
Part Time Jobs and Volunteer Work 77

Chapter 11   Single Parents and Working Parents 79
Your Work Schedule 80
Family and Friends 80
Older Children 81
Work-at-Home Possibilities 81

Chapter 12   The Juggling Act: Housework and Homeschool 83
Prioritizing for Maximum Efficiency 83
Chores 84
Laundry 86
Meals 87
Other Tips 89

Chapter 13   Staying Motivated and Preventing Burnout 90
Setting Goals 91
Get Your Children Excited About Learning 91
How to Make Learning Fun 92
Handling Sibling Rivalry 94
Discipline 96
Rewards and Consequences 96
Special One-on-One Time 98
Getting Your Students' Best Work 98
Motivating Teenagers 100
Vacations 101

Regular Breaks 101
Creative Outlets and Diversions 102
Internet Groups 103
Marriage and Homeschooling 104
Preventing Teacher Burnout 104

Chapter 14   Socialization: Finding Something for Everyone 107
Homeschool Support Groups 108
Co-ops 109
Field Trips 110
Sports 112
Extracurricular Activities 112
Playgroups 113
Church 114
Neighborhood and Community 114
Friends 115
Additional Socialization Opportunities 116

Conclusion **117**

Bibliography **119**

Index **125**

Acknowledgments

Once again, I thank my husband, Tim, and my four children, Megan, Ashley, Zachary, and Windsor. Tim has always been supportive and encouraging, and my children have been so understanding when their mom spent hours at the computer "working on her book."

In writing this book, I owe a great deal to the many works by authors acknowledged in the Bibliography. Thanks are also due to countless homeschooling parents who have shared their advice and favorite tips with me through emails and personal discussions. Specifically, I thank the members of the Elmore County Homeschool Organization (ECHO). Through the monthly parents' discussions at ECHO, I have learned so many time-saving tips and teaching techniques and gathered practical information for this book.

In particular, I appreciate the help of three homeschooling moms who have been gracious and giving despite their demanding schedules: Victoria Lofgren, homeschooling mother of seven; Anita Ottinger, homeschooling mom of four; and Pam Olson, homeschooling mom of three. Thank you for answering all my questions and elaborating in detail your own homeschooling experiences.

I truly appreciate the creative talents of Marty McIntyre, who designed the cover, and Anita Ottinger, who took all the photographs. Finally, I thank my editing team, LaLonni Mizzell, Amy Tanner, Angie Brailsford, and Rochelle Andrews, for reading and proofing the manuscript. Your constructive comments have helped me focus the book in a way that I could not have done on my own.

Introduction

Carren and Tim have always homeschooled their four children.

Another mom called me this morning with questions about homeschool legalities in our state and how to get started. I reassured her and explained what to do. She asked a few questions, getting more enthusiastic and excited with each answer, before saying, "I have three children, and I'm planning to homeschool our youngest child. I would love to homeschool all of them, but I just don't think I can. *How do you homeschool more than one child?*"

How do I answer that question? We homeschool four children, and many families I know successfully homeschool four children and even more. Anita has four children, Shelley has five, Bonnie has six, and Victoria has seven, just to name only four that I know personally. I look at them in amazement sometimes. How *do* they homeschool several children successfully?

Just as each family is different, each homeschooling family has its own unique method for success. As for me, I am a list-maker. I am rather organized, or as my husband fondly says, "anal retentive." I make lists about everything because I have a bad memory. Four children will do that to you. In this book, I share my lists with you. As a homeschooling mom of more than one child, you likely do not have time to weed through extraneous information that may or may not apply to your situation. On the other hand, you probably do have time to highlight quick tips and long-term strategies for handling a variety of situations you will likely face as you homeschool more than one child, especially if those tips and strategies have worked for others.

However, this book includes more than lists. After all, not everything can be listed neatly, particularly when dealing with children. Plus, list-making is not a requirement for homeschooling successfully. If you are not a list-maker, you will still benefit from the tips and techniques in this book because they all relate specifically to families with more than one child.

Who This Book Is For

Homeschoolers with more than one child face a unique situation. Unlike parents with a single child, we must juggle the academic needs of each individual child while at the same time organize the required paperwork, gather books and materials, plan field trips, find extracurricular activities—not just for one, but for two, three, four or more children at once! Additionally, we often must do so with the same limited space, time and finances as those of parents with only one child. This book addresses those unique concerns. This guide is for you and for other parents who need help getting started or who desire fresh ideas for homeschooling more than one child.

Homeschooling More Than One Child: A Practical Guide for Families contains answers to questions I have been asked over the years. These answers are based on my experiences with homeschooling four children and on lengthy discussions with families who have homeschooled even more children for longer than I have. It also includes information gathered from numerous resources. As a result, you should find the information sound and helpful.

This book is not a warm and fuzzy collection of stories. Rather, it is a sensible reference for homeschooling information, tips and strategies for families of any size on any budget. Whether you plan a traditional, eclectic or unschooling approach, this book will help you:

- Get started and meet state requirements
- Organize your time, records, and materials
- Modify or design a curriculum to suit more than one child
- Use the Internet and free software to make homeschooling easy and affordable
- Balance the needs of different ages and abilities
- Occupy babies, toddlers, and preschoolers when you need to teach older kids
- Tackle homeschooling as a single parent or working parent
- Get housework done while homeschooling

- Keep your children motivated
- Prevent teacher burnout
- Handle the inevitable sibling rivalry
- Find socialization opportunities that appeal to multiple ages and interests

Whether you homeschool two children or ten, have ample funds or a limited budget, the tips and strategies in this book will give you the confidence you need to continue homeschooling all your children or to start homeschooling your first grader even though you still have two in diapers. Homeschoolers in every stage will find pertinent information, from tips on handling toddlers while teaching older children to advice on juggling the academic needs of preschoolers, middle schoolers, and high schoolers simultaneously.

How To Use This Book

Homeschooling More Than One Child: A Practical Guide for Families is an organized, step-by-step approach to homeschooling with an emphasis on multiple children. It covers issues that a homeschooler of more than one child may face from the time a family starts to homeschool until that family graduates the last student. To get the most from this book, you may want to read it from beginning to end; indeed, it is written with the idea that once you get started, you choose a curriculum next, and then gather supplies, then work on a schedule, etc.

However, given the nature of homeschooling, some topics overlap chapters. For example, the sections on selecting a curriculum for multiple children may be found in "The Right Curriculum to Suit Each Child" as well as in "The Penny-Pinching Homeschooler: Affording Materials on One Income." As a result, you should be able to find solid answers to your questions without worrying that you may miss vital information by jumping around the chapters.

Sure, you could surf the Internet for homeschool articles or discuss home-school topics in a forum, but the results may be difficult to retain and hard to take along with you. Besides, I have already done the research for you! This book encapsulates information on homeschooling multiple children and provides practical advice and helpful lists right at your fingertips. Take it with you, consult it at a moment's notice, and highlight the parts you want to remember.

As with other homeschooling books, keep what fits your family and leave the rest. After all, each homeschool experience is unique. All the tips that work for my family may not work for yours. Whether you are a new homeschooler or a veteran, you can use the ideas as they are, or use them as a springboard to find the best for your family.

Chapter 1

Getting Started: Jumping In With Both Feet

Start the school year by reading aloud from a good book and gradually adding other subjects every couple of weeks.

Rather than think of homeschooling in terms of starting a new endeavor, think in terms of continuing something you have been doing since your children were born! After all, who helped them learn to walk, talk, brush their teeth, and use good manners? You probably also taught them colors, numbers, and the alphabet. In effect, you have been teaching your children from the time they were babies, often with all of them learning new skills at different levels at the same time. Home education is simply an extension of that.

Don't worry if one child already goes to preschool or if your tenth grader attends public school. You can homeschool your children, whether you have two or ten, and the process of starting is very simple. Whether your children have never been in a formal academic setting or you have to withdraw one or more from school, follow these five steps to start your homeschooling adventure.

Step 1: Think, Discuss, and Decide

Think about your reasons for homeschooling and discuss options with your spouse. Pray about your decision together. Although starting to homeschool is the simplest part of the process, homeschooling itself should not be entered into lightly. It takes a real commitment. Homeschooling is a lifestyle, not a quick fix to a problem. Be sure you understand why you want to homeschool and that both of you agree that it is the best choice for your family.

Step 2: Find Out About State Regulations

Home education is legal in the United States, but each state has its own regulations. Therefore, once you decide to homeschool, find out the laws in your state, specifically the age at which a child must be officially in school. If one of your children is compulsory age, then you must follow state regulations. However, if your children are not yet compulsory age, you have time to become comfortable with teaching at home before meeting any regulations.

Because laws vary from state to state and are subject to change, each state's regulations are not covered here. Instead, contact a local support group, check the library, or search online for information during the summer so you will not miss any deadlines. A great Web site for the laws in each state is the Home School Legal Defense Association at www.HSLDA.org. Do not contact your local public or private schools, school superintendent or board of education. They may not keep abreast of the latest changes to homeschool regulations and may inadvertently give you misleading information as a result.

You should research the following regulations:

- Compulsory school age, which is the age that the law requires your child to be in school.
- Legal options, such as registering with the school superintendent or filing a legal affidavit.
- Subjects required.
- Attendance, meaning the number of days required for a school year.
- Teacher qualifications, such as a high school diploma or teacher certification.

- Record keeping, such as grades or portfolios.
- Testing, such as annual tests you can administer yourself or state standardized tests.

Once you research the state regulations, you may start homeschooling as soon as it feels right for your family. If you wish to follow the school calendar year, start in the fall. If your children cannot wait to open those new books you just purchased, then start in the middle of summer! If one or all of your children are in school now, you do not have to wait until the school year ends to remove them from the system. Contact a local homeschool support group or the Home School Legal Defense Association (HSLDA) to find out the proper procedure in your state for withdrawing a child from school mid-year.

Step 3: Find a Support Group

Although you do not need a support group to homeschool successfully, your best interest would be to join one. If you seek support in your education efforts and want homeschool friends for your children, then you will find a support group valuable. Furthermore, the group leaders can answer your questions and direct you to someone who has handled situations similar to yours. For example, they can explain the process of withdrawing a child from public school, suggest a curriculum, and introduce you to another parent who homeschools a gifted or learning-disabled child. They will also keep you updated on any changes to state homeschool laws. For information on finding or starting a group, refer to Chapter 14.

Step 4: Choose a Curriculum

Your next step will likely be to select a curriculum. So many resources are available that this may be the most difficult part of getting started, but it's difficult only because of the quantity and variety available. Styles vary from the structured packaged program to the relaxed unschooling style, with everything in between. Don't worry—one style is not better than any other. What works in your family is the best way.

Unless your state requires curriculum approval, you do not have to make a decision right away, and you can always change your mind. The best advice is to research your options. For details on choosing or designing a curriculum to fit each child, refer to Chapter 3.

Step 5: Use Available Resources

Homeschool seminars and conventions provide information and inspiration for the homeschooling family, so check with local support groups for upcoming events. Also, representatives from most curriculum companies attend large conferences, allowing you to ask questions, view their products, and order materials at a discount.

Other valuable resources include the library and Internet. After you decide to homeschool, read everything you can find on home education. Ask the librarian to help you find magazines and books. Surf the Internet for Web sites; start with a search on "homeschool" and follow the links. Talk with homeschooling families. All of these resources will provide you with other points of view and may present options you may not have considered.

Transitioning to Homeschooling

Plan a transition period to help you and your children get used to homeschooling. Our family did not start homeschooling with a house full of children. We had time to get used to homeschooling, one student at a time. By the time we became accustomed to homeschooling a single child, it was time to start homeschooling our second child, and then our third child was born. As we were homeschooling our two oldest children, our fourth child was born. Finally, after we grew accustomed to homeschooling three children, it was time to start educating our fourth child. Just as we did not suddenly have four children at once, we did not suddenly homeschool four children at once. We had time to adjust.

You, too, will find a gradual adjustment to be the easiest method. If you already have two or more children to homeschool at once, you can still start gradually: Teach only one subject for two weeks and add another subject every week or two. Especially if you have pulled your children from a traditional school, give them a few weeks to relax, grow accustomed to the new wake-up schedule and chore routines, and make the transition from institutional school to home school. This will also give you time to adjust to homeschooling more than one child. Of course, if you live in a high regulation state, you may not have the luxury of several weeks to adjust to homeschool. Be sure you know the law in your state, and use whatever time you have.

Whether you have a few days or several weeks, here are a few more tips to make the most of this adjustment time for all of you:

- **Go to the library once a week.** Whether your children check out books or not, take home some books that your children would find interesting and place them out in the open. Include reading books at various levels and coffee-table books with pictures. Select a book to read aloud to everyone. Also, meet the librarians and learn to use the library's computer system.

- **Prepare a storage area and start gathering basic school supplies.** You may need to reorganize your home to make room.
- **Set up a tentative schedule of daily and weekly chores, housework, and errands.** Keep the television off during the day or allow only limited access.
- **Find out what your children are interested in before choosing a curriculum.** Not only will this help you organize your thoughts on how to proceed, but also it will get them excited about learning.
- **Talk with your children a lot.** After a while, your children will grow accustomed to discussing issues with you in a comfortable environment and to thinking outside of the box. No more pat, rehearsed answers! If you must grade assignments, grade only those with obvious right or wrong answers, such as math.

This decompression time will also give you a chance to feel your way and adjust to homeschooling as well. Just think, no more 6 a.m. alarm clocks! No more car pool lines! No more homework! No more wondering if—and what—your children are learning!

Chapter 2

For the Record: Organizing the Paperwork

*Older students can maintain their own records
with some supervision from their parents.*

Keeping records for several children may seem like an overwhelming task, especially if your state requires extensive documentation. However, the task is much easier if you maintain a certain place for records, color-code them by child, train your children to help you, and keep track of activities as they are completed. Waiting until the last minute does not work well for one child, much less for several children.

How detailed your records need to be depends on state requirements. A home-school support group can provide information or direct you to the proper source.

No matter what your state requires, you need copies of your children's school records from any public or private school they previously attended. If your children have never attended a formal school, then start keeping records yourself. Be sure to have copies of their health and immunization records by contacting their pediatrician or local health department for the necessary forms.

Reasons for Keeping Records

The main reason for keeping records is to meet state requirements. If ever questioned, your records will prove that you have been educating your children. Even if your state does not require records, however, you will find them helpful. Keeping records will make the transition easier if your children ever have to go to school, even temporarily, or if you move to another state that requires detailed records. Needless to say, good records will also help your children get into good colleges and earn scholarships.

Another reason for keeping records is for your own peace of mind. Records document learning. How else will you know if your methods are working unless you keep track of what you are doing? Daily work journals and samples of work show progress. For example, we keep samples of each child's handwriting at the beginning of the school year. At the end of the year, we compare those samples to recent handwriting assignments to show each child the progress he has made. We also use essays and timed math assignments for our junior high and high school students. The obvious improvements not only reassure us and other family members of their progress but also motivate our children to continue.

Best of all, records can be used to customize a homeschooling program to fit each child. You will be able to look back and see what worked with an older child and decide if duplicating your methods will work with a younger child. You can also note that certain methods or books did not work out as well, so you may want to use different materials for your next child. As a result, consider keeping some type of records even if not required.

Record-keeping Methods

As long as you meet state requirements, you can choose any record-keeping method that fits your family. If you use a conventional curriculum and a traditional teaching approach, you will likely favor traditional record-keeping methods, such as lesson plans and study charts. On the other hand, if your family's approach to education is different from that of traditional schools or you unschool, you may prefer to keep a journal or a scrapbook so you can document learning not traditionally related to academics. Besides conventional subjects and field trips, you may want to record computer use, games, cooking, travel, theater, museums, educational videos and television programs, arts and crafts, music lessons, dance classes, athletics, volunteer work, scouting, and church activities.

Of course, you can always combine various record-keeping methods in a unique approach that fits your individual family. Just remember that keeping records should not interfere with learning, but should support it, so don't become a slave to your record-keeping. If you find it becoming a burden, whatever method you use, change it.

Depending on how detailed you need or want to be, here are some record-keeping methods with tips on how to accommodate multiple children easily:

- *Assignment book.* In an assignment book, you write each child's assignments and grades. Each child can keep an assignment book or you can maintain a single book for all your children. If you use one book, allocate a different color pen for each child or divide the book into sections for each child with labeled tabs for easy organization.

- *Attendance.* Use an attendance sheet, teacher's attendance book, or a calendar to mark school days. Some curricula include instructor's guides with each day broken down into lessons; simply check off or date each assignment upon completion for a record of attendance.

- *Book List.* You may want to maintain a list of books that each child reads. Record the title and author at least, but you may also want to record the date your child finished reading the book.

- *Course of Study.* A course of study is a list of subjects to be taught and materials to be used. Use labeled tabs to separate each child's section. Alternatively, have specific subjects sectioned with each child's coursework listed by color.

- *Grades.* To figure a grade, divide the number of correct questions by the total number of questions. Multiply this number by 100 to turn it into a percentage. A suggested basic grading scale is 90-100% = A; 80-89% = B; 70-79% = C; 60-69% = D; below 60% = F. For a tougher course, use 93-100% = A; 85-92% = B; 77-84% = C; 70-76% = D; below 70% = F. For letter grades, A is excellent, B is above average, C is average, D is below average, and F is fail.

- *Journal.* Many parents document everything their children do each day in a journal. Not only do they write down completed assignments and note any areas for improvement, but they also include character developments and non-academic pursuits that could be considered educational. Some parents keep a spiral notebook by their bed to jot down additional activities or accomplishments that they may otherwise forget by the next day.

- *Lesson Plan.* A lesson plan is an outline of activities, what should be learned, the resources to be used and how to use them. Most curriculum companies provide lesson plans with their materials. You can also find free lesson plans online. Color-code by child as needed.

- *Notebooking.* This method encourages a student to creatively collect information in a notebook, which he may then use for review or for a portfolio. The student usually creates a different notebook for each subject or topic rather than one notebook for the year.

- *Portfolio.* Because a portfolio is a representative sample of each child's work for the year, not a collection of all of his work, save everything throughout the year in separate containers and decide later what will actually be included. Consider items such as completed worksheets and workbooks, book lists, science notebooks, research papers, reports, and photographs of field trips and projects. Don't forget drawings, ticket stubs, brochures, and souvenirs. Be sure to include any mandated items if your state requires a portfolio.

- *Record Keeping Systems.* Many systems are available to purchase or use online and provide a convenient method and location for paperwork. Homeschool Tracker may be found at www.tghomesoft.com. Free calendars and forms may be found at www.DonnaYoung.org, www.PrintFree.com and www.Homeschooling.About.com. If they do not have what you need, search for "homeschool forms" or "homeschool record keeping" online.

- *Report Card or Progress Report.* While a report card shows grades in each subject, a progress report generally details improvements in traditional subjects as well as in non-academic areas, such as hobbies and character virtues.

- *Scope and Sequence.* A scope and sequence is a list of topics and skills that a student learns in a particular grade. Many curriculum companies use their own scope and sequence, so if you purchase a packaged curriculum you will be following that company's scope and sequence. Of course, you can always design your own.

- *Scrapbook.* Some families have each child create a scrapbook of the year. The child includes photos of projects and field trips, artwork, samples of his work, and family events.

- *Study Chart.* Set up a one-page study chart with assignments to do each day. Use a different color for each child, and let each child put a check mark or sticker on completed assignments. This allows you to see instantly what has been done and who may need help.

- *To-Do List.* You can prepare a to-do list for each child either daily or weekly. You or they check off completed assignments and then add any unplanned events that occur. The to-do list will not only keep students focused, but will also serve as a record of their work.

- *Transcript.* A transcript is a list of subjects, the grades received, and the units each course is worth. If you unschool, translate what your children learn into educational terms, such as math and science.

Organizing Records for Multiple Students

You can devise your own record-keeping system on your home computer. Use a word processor to maintain book lists and a spreadsheet to keep grades. Since your children will be studying the same topics and subjects, you can easily cut and paste the necessary information from one child's document to another. Be sure to save back-ups periodically to prevent losing data. As an extra precaution, you may want to print out hard copies, color-code them by child, and keep them in a filing cabinet or storage box with a lid.

Better yet, have your older children maintain their own records, with some supervision from you. Victoria, homeschooling mother of seven, keeps records for her younger children on a day-to-day basis, while her junior high and high school students do their own record-keeping for themselves on a chart. Quarterly, she evaluates what they have been doing and where they are heading to ensure that they stay on track.

Regardless of the method you use, consistency is important, especially for more than one child. Maintain records as you go rather than rush around at the end of the quarter trying to remember what each child did several weeks ago. For more tips on organizing and storing your records, refer to Chapter 5.

Chapter 3

The Right Curriculum To Suit Each Child

Choosing a curriculum can be a difficult decision
simply because of the variety of materials available.

A homeschool curriculum varies from a structured packaged program to a relaxed unschooling style, with all sorts of options in between. One style is not better than another. What works for your children is the best way, whether you purchase a complete package or create your own. You can even design a custom curriculum tailored to each child's needs. Sounds intimidating? It does not have to be. This chapter will help you organize your thoughts on the best approach for the students in your family.

Teaching Methods and Styles

Before you consider what you need in a curriculum, you should know the different kinds available, the teaching styles they advocate, and the advantages and disadvantages often associated with them. Although some methods work better for teaching multiple children than others, you should choose the method that would be best for your family. You can even combine methods to ensure a well-rounded education.

Here are brief descriptions of different approaches:

- *Charlotte Mason.* Charlotte Mason was an 1800's educator who advocated minimal academics and more time to explore nature and the fine arts. Families following the Charlotte Mason method read classics aloud and have their children narrate back, spend a lot of time in nature, and allow each child to pursue his own interests. As a result, this method requires significant time from the parent in reading and helping each child pursue his interests.

- *Classical.* Often referred to as the Trivium, this method includes such subjects as logic, philosophy, Greek, and Latin. Parents who use the Classical Approach try to develop independent thinking and logical analysis in their children, rather than merely teach subjects. As a result, the course load can be rather demanding on both students and parents.

- *Correspondence Schools.* A correspondence school, or "distance learning," provides all the resources needed by a student for a school year. He will complete the lessons, mail or email them to an instructor, receive grades, and graduate to the next grade level at the end of the year. Some are even accredited. However, because the student must complete all lessons, this method will not be very flexible for more than one student.

- *CD-ROMs.* Many curriculum companies offer courses on CD-ROMs, and you can find educational games and software in nearly all subjects. Many parents like this option because their children consider them play rather than work. Also, in this digital age, parents agree that the more exposure to computers a child has, the better. However, invest wisely because CD-ROMs can be expensive. Get recommendations from other parents, and be sure the software will work on your computer before you purchase it.

- *Eclectic.* Many homeschoolers consider their approach to be eclectic because they pick and choose among various methods and different curriculum companies to customize a program to fit each child's needs. They may purchase a history textbook from one company, a phonics workbook from another company, and a science program from still a third company. While it may mean extra work for you in selecting the materials and coordinating the lesson plans, it is generally not as time-consuming as designing your own curriculum from scratch.

- *Literature-Based.* Literature-based curricula focus on the classics and great works of modern literature. Many parents prefer this method because, instead of textbooks, they have quality books in their home libraries that will appeal to their children for pleasure reading again and again. However, a literature-based curriculum may not be the best choice for students who dislike reading, struggle with reading or have little spare time for reading.

- *Textbooks.* Because most history and science textbooks condense information very well and explain concepts logically, they can be read aloud to several grade levels at once, which is ideal for families with more than one child. However, some students find textbooks boring, and sometimes the information may be misleading or give a biased opinion. For example, many science books may present evolution as fact rather than as theory and may not include a creation point of view. Also, many world history books view history from a western mindset and barely mention eastern accomplishments.

- *Unit Studies.* With unit studies, children learn several subjects at once while studying one particular topic or theme. You can find unit study plans on the Internet and in books, or you can design your own. Some Web sites even explain how to plan a unit study. Many families use unit studies to teach several grade levels at once. Since this method usually includes many hands-on activities, unit studies can be fun. However, compared to workbooks and textbooks, unit studies require a lot of work for parents to prepare and carry out the activities.

- *Unschooling.* Unschoolers use neither a prepared curriculum nor a scope and sequence. Instead, they pursue each child's interests as they arise, which is why unschooling is often termed "child-led learning," "delight-directed learning," and "natural learning." Unschoolers believe that, because children naturally love to learn, they will learn what they need from everyday life and through the pursuit of their interests. This method requires a great deal of parental involvement in helping each student find resources and information on subjects he wants to pursue. Also, it may be difficult to convey adequately what an unschooler does into a transcript for college.

- *Videos and DVDs.* Many curriculum companies provide video courses in which an actual teacher explains the material step-by-step. Your students can review sections over and over if necessary. While some parents like having a professional explain difficult math or science concepts, others dislike the lack of interaction between students and instructor.

- *Workbooks.* Workbooks appeal to children and parents, too. Students can write in the books and take them anywhere. Because most workbooks are self-explanatory, students can work independently. However, some parents consider workbooks to be mostly "busy work."

Family Issues to Consider

Now that you know more about the different kinds of curricula available, you are well on the way to making an informed decision for your family. As a homeschooling parent of more than one child, you need a curriculum that makes it easy to teach several grade levels at once and enables students to work on their own. Mindful of these two necessities, answer the following questions before making a decision:

1. **What are your educational goals?** You need goals so you will know what your children are accomplishing and if your curriculum is working. Focus on what you want to achieve by the end of the academic year. Generally, your goals will relate to why you are homeschooling, and you may have a different one for each child. For example, if you want one child to learn to read, you will need a language arts curriculum that focuses on teaching a child to read in one year. If you want high school students to earn academic college scholarships, then you need a college-prep curriculum.

2. **What do you want your students to learn?** For instance, you may want to study world history this year or include life skills or use a Christian-based curriculum. For guidance, consult the scope and sequence plans from various curriculum companies or the course of study at www.WorldBook.com.

3. **How much money do you want to spend?** A packaged curriculum may be expensive, so you may want to create your own to save money.

4. **How much time do you want to invest?** Some curricula require a lot of preparation and involvement from the parent, while others allow students to work independently. Also, designing your own curriculum will require more preparation than purchasing one with materials and lesson plans already included.

5. **What are your children's learning styles and current interests?** One child may do well with workbooks, while another needs hands-on activities, and yet another one loves to read. Furthermore, if one child is currently fasci-

nated by outer space, for example, you may want to find a science curriculum that covers astronomy.

6. **What subjects will be taught across grade levels?** As long as they are within a few grades of each other, children can share history, science, foreign language, and Bible.

Once you have answered these questions, you will be more likely to find or design a curriculum that fits your family just right.

Purchasing a Curriculum for Multiple Ages

Not only are you teaching different grades, but your students are most likely at different levels among subjects as well. Most third graders, for example, are not usually at the third grade level in all subjects. While you can buy a separate curriculum for each child, you may become overwhelmed with the day-to-day task of implementing several different curricula at once.

Instead, search for a flexible and reusable curriculum that teaches multiple children at different levels and enables individual work. Heart of Wisdom, KONOS, Robinson, Sonlight, Tapestry of Grace, TRISMS, and Weaver are popular with large families in our homeschool group, but many others may easily be modified for multiple children. Keep in mind, however, that no one has written the perfect curriculum that will meet your family's unique needs. You will have to modify your chosen curriculum in some ways to make it suitable for your family.

Modifying an older student's program for younger students will be easier than making a program more challenging for older students. Therefore, choose a curriculum that fits the needs of your oldest child first, particularly if he is in high school, and adapt it to younger children by adding easier books and activities geared to their abilities. For students up to elementary grades, focus on reading, writing, and math. Add additional subjects as they get older.

Packaged curricula appeal to some families because they are usually easy to implement and include all the supplies needed for a school year. Teacher's manuals explain the concepts, and lesson plans are easy to follow. Also, staying with the same curriculum over the years saves time and energy because learning to teach a new curriculum requires a great deal of effort. You also save money when you reuse materials with each subsequent child.

However, you may decide that one curriculum company does not meet the needs of all your children the way you would like. Instead, you may be partial to the history from one company and the language arts program from another company, or one child may do better with workbooks while another child needs hands-on activities. By all means, search for materials that are suited to each individual child no matter where you find them.

Finding the Right Curriculum

Homeschooling parents use different methods to find the right curriculum for their children. Some go strictly by popularity, using curricula favored by their homeschooling friends and local private schools. In fact, if you have just withdrawn your children from school, you can finish the year with the curriculum the school has been using. Similarly, if you plan for one or all of your children to go to a private school eventually, using the same curriculum as the school will make the adjustment easier for your children.

However, this does not mean that the curriculum will actually suit your children. The best way to determine if certain resources will meet your children's needs is to review the materials, talk with other parents who use them, and include your children in your research. Check the curriculum companies' Web sites because most of them have descriptions and photos of their products. Also, you can call, email or write for their catalogs for free.

Here are suggestions to help you research and find the right curriculum for your children:

- **Homeschool conferences and fairs often have booths for vendors.** You can view samples, ask questions, and order materials. Keep in mind, however, that salesmen will present their products in the best possible light.
- **Homeschool support groups often maintain a supply of catalogs and samples.** Even small groups may ask members to bring samples for others to examine during meetings.
- **Bookstores usually carry homeschool resources and may even have a homeschool section.** Although you will be unable to ask questions from someone who has used the materials, at least you will be able to skim through the books before you purchase them.
- **Go to the library.** You can look over the books that the library happens to have, see if you might find them useful, and then go to a store to buy what you want.
- **Some homeschool books provide detailed descriptions about available curricula, including costs, advantages, and disadvantages.** Check out Mary Pride's *Big Book of Home Learning* and Cathy Duffy's *The Christian Home Educator's Curriculum Manual*.

- **Online homeschool forums provide several opinions in one spot at one time.** Ask questions and read about what others use in homeschool email groups.
- **Read reviews of individual books posted by previous consumers at such online bookstores as www.Amazon.com and www.BarnesAndNoble.com.** The comments may help you even if you decide not to purchase books from these sites.

You can ask other homeschoolers and look around, but when making a choice on a curriculum, you must make the decision, no one else. Go with your gut feelings because you know your children better than any teacher or any other homeschooling parent. Besides, you are not making an irrevocable decision; you can always sell the materials and buy something else if they do not work for your children.

Supplementing Your Curriculum

Sometimes you may find a lack in your chosen curriculum. It may not cover subjects that you want your children to learn, or its coverage may just scratch the surface, or one child may not understand the concepts as that curriculum presents them. Whether or not you use a boxed program, you can supplement and reinforce learning with a variety of materials and options.

The library and Internet provide valuable supplements for homeschoolers, and even television offers unexpected resources. Go to the Web site for Cable in the Classroom at www.ciconline.com, and check local listings for educational channels such as PBS, A&E, History Channel, Biography Channel, Discovery Channel, and The Learning Channel (TLC). Have blank tapes available to record episodes you may want to use later or those that air in the wee hours of the morning; you may want to invest in TiVo to record programs. Also, many of these channels offer free lesson plans on their Web sites to go along with their programs.

Here are other potential supplements for your curriculum:

- Educational videos and DVDs
- Educational games and software
- Encyclopedia study guides
- Local experts and retired teachers
- Workbooks from supermarkets and discount stores
- Hands-on activities, projects, and experiments

- Games such as Uno® (numbers and matching), Yahtzee® (math), Monopoly® (math), Scrabble® (spelling and vocabulary), chess (strategy), and checkers (strategy)
- Museums, zoos, planetariums, aquariums, and ecological parks
- Historic sites, living history days, and festivals
- Co-ops through homeschool groups and umbrella schools
- Classes through community centers and colleges

Teaching Required Subjects

States vary on required academic subjects, so consult your state regulations. Most packaged curricula include materials for traditional subjects. Besides a packaged program, you can find other methods to meet subject requirements. Try these suggestions:

- *Art.* Check with local artists, community centers, and colleges for art classes. On your own, introduce your children to the great artists by displaying a few works of one artist over a period of time. Print them from the Internet or cut them out of calendars. Every so often, discuss them with your children. Then rotate them out for another set by another artist.
- *Bible.* Nothing beats reading directly from the Bible. Various study guides, workbooks, and activity books supplement reading. Online lesson plans and activities are also available. Go to www.eSword.com or search on "Bible lesson plans."
- *Drama.* If your city has a community theatre, volunteer backstage. If tickets are cost-prohibitive, check on free or low-cost dress rehearsals. Some churches and homeschool groups organize plays, drama clubs, and classes with local actors as teachers. Look for classes through local theatres, community centers, and colleges. At the very least, encourage any budding actors to dramatize favorite stories and historical events for the family at home.
- *Driver's Education.* Homeschool driving programs provide the necessary paperwork as well as videos and online instruction. Check out www.DriverEdTraining.com, www.DriverzEd.com, and www.National DriverTraining.com. You could also enroll your teen in a local driving school; check the yellow pages for listings. However, find out state laws and automobile insurance requirements before you order or enroll in a program.
- *Foreign Languages.* Engage a private instructor, or learn along with your children by using computer software and games, free online lessons, audio

cassettes and CDs, and storybooks written in the language you are studying.

- *History, Literature, and Language Arts.* Volumes of interesting books and workbooks are available. You can always read from the classics to expose children to great stories from history as well as good writing and new vocabulary in context. Go online for lessons and watch historical programs on television. Use the library. Join a book club. Also, have your students write or narrate stories to you. Being able to narrate stories aloud eventually progresses to being able to write them down.

- *Home Economics and Health.* These subjects can be taught during the context of daily life by having your children help clean the house, do laundry, and cook meals. Various books are also available, and lesson plans may be found online.

- *Math.* Teacher's manuals explain complicated math concepts. Games and Web sites can be used to introduce and reinforce math concepts. Also, take advantage of real life opportunities, such as shopping and budgeting.

- *Music.* Investigate private lessons, city youth symphonies, musical productions, church choirs, and music competitions. Check the yellow pages and consult your local homeschool group. On your own, focus on a different composer each month. Have your children listen to recordings of Mozart or Beethoven while they help you cook, fold laundry, and run errands.

- *Physical Education.* Not all athletics are affiliated with public schools. Try the local YCMA, fitness gym, city recreation department, and community center for swim teams, soccer leagues, gymnastics teams as well as T-ball, softball, and football. Many churches sponsor Upward sports ministries in basketball, soccer, and cheerleading. Depending on where you live, your family can hike, bicycle, surf, sail, water-ski, snowboard, and snow ski. Check the yellow pages for sports-related businesses, such as golf, martial arts, archery, and horseback riding. In addition, many homeschool groups organize sports and physical education classes. You can also find books appropriate for a family P.E. class, such as *The Ultimate Homeschool Physical Education Game Book* by Guy Bailey.

- *Science.* Read science books and do experiments. Have your children keep nature notebooks with drawings of insects and samples of leaves. Several Web sites focus on science topics, as do television programs like "Bill Nye, The Science Guy" and "The Magic School Bus" and science channels like Noggin. Also, support groups often organize co-op classes, and some community colleges offer science classes and workshops.

Designing Your Own Curriculum

You can certainly design your own curriculum from the start. Tailoring a curriculum to fit each child is one of the benefits of homeschooling, and many families enjoy the challenges and rewards of such an endeavor. A customized curriculum promises flexibility and financial savings. On the other hand, it will cost you in terms of hours of preparation because you will be the one to write the lesson plans, search for books, and gather necessary supplies.

Creating your own curriculum may sound like an overwhelming task if you have several children, but it is not as difficult as you may think with the library and Internet at your disposal. A curriculum is simply a plan of what will be studied. If you do not know where to start, you can find typical courses of study from books such as *What Your Child Needs to Know When* by Robin Sampson and the series that includes *What Your Third Grader Needs To Know* by E.D. Hirsch, Jr. Many families use them as guidelines and then supplement with the library and Internet as needed. You can also find scope and sequence plans online. For example, www.WorldBook.com provides a typical course of study for preschool through grade 12.

You may want to use workbooks that discount stores carry for different grade levels. They cover the typical subjects for lower grades in one convenient workbook. Some homeschoolers use them as guidelines and supplement with additional books, games, computer software, and videos. On the other hand, you may want to teach what you feel is important and let your children learn what they want to learn. After all, one of the benefits of homeschooling is the flexibility that allows each child to explore his own interests at his own pace.

When creating a curriculum from scratch, start the same way as you would if you were purchasing a curriculum. Cater to your oldest student's needs, and modify the curriculum to fit younger children. If your oldest child has not yet studied American history, for example, focus on American history with books and materials for his level. For younger children, add books at lower levels and activities that will interest them that are geared to American history.

Search the Internet for topics and resources. You can do a general search on "history workbooks" or "history lesson plans," or you can be more specific by searching on "Pilgrim lesson plans." Investigate the links that show up and decide which ones you want to pursue. Keep notes of the Web site links and recommended books, and make copies of the lesson plans.

For example, when designing a year-long curriculum on our state history, I looked online for a state history timeline. Using the timeline as a guide, I searched for free lesson plans and activities related to the topics and geared to each grade level of my children. From there, field trips, virtual field trips and books related to the people, places, and events listed in the timeline were included. After breaking down the topics into monthly and weekly lessons and activities and finding the curriculum too short, I added special holiday activities to lengthen the course to fit our school year.

You, too, can design your own curriculum. Follow these steps:

1. **Determine what you want your children to learn.** Follow a scope and sequence or choose a subject, theme or topic on your own.

2. **Surf the Internet.** Numerous Web sites offer free lesson plans, worksheets, book lists, projects, experiments, songs, coloring pages, games, and crafts to go with your topic or theme. Use your favorite search engine to find them. As you gather resources, set up a file for your notes as well as favorites folders on your browser for Web sites. Either note the Web site address so you can come back when you are ready to use it, or print the materials now, just in case the site may not be functioning by the time you need it.

3. **Find related field trips.** Use the Internet, yellow pages, and chambers of commerce for locations. If you cannot find sites related to the topic, simply explore your community or search online for virtual field trips.

4. **Plan each month and/or week.** Include an estimated length of time to complete the lessons as well as all the resources and activities and where to find them.

5. **Make a list of needed materials and books.** On a monthly or weekly basis, refer to the list to gather the necessary supplies.

Knowing What to Teach

Beginning homeschoolers, whether they purchase a curriculum or create their own, often ask, "How do you know what to teach?" Curriculum companies use a scope and sequence that determines what is taught in which grade. If you purchase a packaged curriculum, then you automatically will follow that company's scope and sequence, and you will not have to worry about missing the fundamentals.

If you design your own curriculum, you can find several scope and sequence books that explain grade by grade what a child should study. As mentioned earlier, *What Your Child Needs to Know When* by Robin Sampson and the series that includes *What Your Third Grader Needs To Know* by E.D. Hirsch, Jr. are two examples, but many others are available. Ask your librarian for help. Also, www.WorldBook.com provides a typical course of study for preschoolers through grade 12. Just remember that every scope and sequence is different, so do not feel you must follow one exactly. Simply use it as a guide. With homeschooling, each child can learn different subjects at different grade levels and can progress when he is ready.

Another frequently asked question is "How do you know you are covering everything?" You will not be able to teach your children all there is to know about history or science. Even the best schools cannot do that because there is just too much for anyone to learn. As a matter of fact, as you teach your children, you will likely come across information that you never remember learning in school. Rather than try to teach them everything, expose them to as much information as possible and teach them the skills they need for a lifestyle of learning. That way, if they discover a gap in their education while in college, for example, they will be able to fill the gap by finding the information they need on their own.

Testing

Another question often asked is "How do you know your children are learning?" You may certainly test if you want. Many curriculum companies provide tests, and some Web sites, such as www.EasyTestMaker.com, offer free test generators online that are easy to set up. Also, standardized tests, such as the Stanford Achievement Test (SAT) and the California Achievement Test (CAT), are regularly administered by support groups and umbrella schools.

However, some tests only show how well students test, not whether they are learning, and your children may not test well. As a homeschooling parent, you will discern if they are learning by your discussions and observations. Ask questions and discuss the material. If you can tell that one student does not understand division, for example, spend more time on it before you teach him fractions. Unlike in a classroom, he does not have to move on until he is ready.

Even so, testing is required in some states, and some parents like tests because they confirm the areas of weakness suspected by the parents. If you test, purchase test prep books to help you prepare your students adequately, and use diagnostic tests instead of achievement tests. The scores from achievement tests are percentile scores comparing your child's results with his age peers. Diagnostic tests, on the other hand, test for basic skills that the child knows or does not know in each subject, which will prove more helpful to you.

Relaxed Homeschooling

Whether you purchase a curriculum or design your own, your homeschooling will become less structured and more relaxed each year. Your ideas will change over time, and sometimes your choices will not work. That's okay! If something does not work, don't stop homeschooling; just change your method or curriculum.

Remember, young children learn from playing, so provide plenty of supplies for creative play, and read to them often. Don't push academics too hard too soon or you all may burn out. If you feel you must use something, purchase workbooks from a discount store and supplement with games, field trips, hands-on activities, and books. Plan to cover the basics in about 30 minutes to an hour each school day, and let your preschooler, kindergartener, first and second graders enjoy being children.

The same goes for your adolescent and teenager. They need time for hobbies, sports, and friends. Let them pursue their own interests. Give them plenty of books to read, supplies for their own projects, and access to resources. Elementary students will spend up to two hours and high school students about three hours each school day on focused school work.

Even if your 15-year-old son does not want to do anything but mechanics, for example, he will still learn a great deal in other areas. He will learn science and math by working on cars. As he looks up information in car manuals, he will practice reading comprehension and research skills. If he is interested in older cars, he may even learn history. As he gets older, he will no doubt recognize the need to learn other subject areas; meanwhile, let him pursue his interest.

No matter what curriculum you use to teach your children or what grades they are in, introduce a new concept or skill as each child shows interest. There is no need to reduce a child to tears over fractions or grammar. If he is not ready, set it aside and then come back a few weeks later. By then, the concept just may click in your child's mind. At the same time, do not hold a child back if he wants to surge ahead. Nothing is stopping your four-year-old from learning to read or your 10-year-old from learning algebra. Indeed, once a child realizes that homeschooling offers the freedom to learn anything, he will want to learn everything that interests him! Encourage him and guide him to the resources he needs.

That is exactly what you are: A guide for your children. You do not have to know everything, or even anything at all, about a subject. Simply guide your children to the resources that will provide the answers, such as a library, local expert or the Internet.

Chapter 4

The Penny-Pinching Homeschooler: Affording Materials on One Income

You do not have to buy materials from a curriculum company to provide quality education for your children.

You can spend as much or as little on educational materials as your budget will allow. Costs vary so much that there is no way to estimate expenses. Literally, you can spend a small fortune or you can school for free. However, whether you are a penny-pincher by nature or by necessity, you can find good bargains without sacrificing quality.

Usability of Packaged Curricula

While a packaged curriculum may be expensive, you may be able to justify the expense if you plan to use it for several children at one time or reuse it for subsequent children. For example, science equipment can be used by several children working on experiments together, and a phonics program can be packed up and used again with each consecutive child.

However, just because you may purchase or already own some type of curriculum does not mean it will be the best option for all your kids. What is right for one child may not be right for another. Instead, meet your children's individual educational needs by using the best materials you can for each child, even if this means you have to put away the expensive phonics program that worked wonderfully for your first, second, and third child but does not work well for the fourth one.

Tips for a Customized Curriculum

Purchasing a packaged curriculum may not be financially practical, especially for a one-income family. Creating your own curriculum will likely be cheaper as well as more rewarding because you can tailor it to suit each child's needs and interests within the confines of your budget. You do not necessarily have to design every aspect of your curriculum. You could create a history course but purchase math from one company, language arts from another company, and science from still another company.

You can even homeschool for free! Use the Internet for free lesson plans, texts, and worksheets. Simply search on the topic, such as "American history lesson plans" or "fraction worksheets," and preface your keywords with "free." The library, too, is a valuable free resource. Get all your books from the local library and use interlibrary loan for books it does not stock.

When designing your own curriculum, consider these tips:

- **Use unit studies to teach multiple students.** A unit study incorporates all subjects in the study of one particular topic. You can purchase unit study packages, create your own, or use free online unit studies. Simply search on the specific topic, such as "Christmas unit studies."
- **Pass down workbooks and lesson plans from child to child.** Take workbooks apart, laminate each page or use page protectors, and place in a binder. Use erasable markers so the pages can be reused. Also, check the copyright notice in workbooks because many allow photocopying for in-home use.

- **Combine related subjects.** Some subjects go well together, such as literature and history, history and geography, or geography and science. Combining subjects saves money on materials, makes teaching easier for you, and helps student retention.
- **Multi-task to conserve limited time.** Read classics or biographies aloud while your children do handwriting or eat lunch. Listen to foreign language CDs when you run errands together.

How To Stay on a Budget

If you need to stay on a limited budget, buy used materials or share a curriculum with another family. To share successfully, the ages of the children must be just right so that you can take turns with the materials each year. When you share, each of you pays for half the cost and buys separate consumables. Teacher's manuals are often the most expensive part of a curriculum, so sharing saves a lot of money. An additional advantage is that many parents gain new ways of teaching a lesson by reading another mom's notes in the used teacher's manuals.

Also, many companies and organizations do not want limited finances to prevent families from benefiting from their products and services, so inquire about grants and scholarships. Many companies offer financial help, as do organizations that sponsor sports camps and similar extracurricular activities.

If you plan to purchase a packaged curriculum or even a mix of books and other resources, these steps will help keep you on a budget:

1. **List the essentials.** These items you cannot do without, such as the next grade level math.
2. **Add the "extras."** Browse curriculum catalogs, Web sites, and online bookstores for resources that you would like to have to supplement your children's education, but don't necessarily need. If you cannot decide between three similar books, put all three on the list for right now.
3. **Prioritize your list.** Consider the learning quality and reusable value as well as price and probable enjoyment for each item. Also, make sure the materials are not similar to supplies you already own. If the total cost exceeds your limit, cross off the items from the bottom of the list or transfer them to a Christmas or birthday wish list. Keep your final list in your purse so you will have it handy when shopping.
4. **Research items to narrow down the list.** Ask around for other opinions and look at samples. Also, check to see how many weeks each book will be used in the curriculum; you may want to purchase books that will be used for sev-

eral months, but borrow or cross off books that will be used for only one or two weeks.

5. **Shop around to find the best prices before actually ordering or buying anything.** Check with Christian Book Distributors (CBD), and compare prices among curriculum companies, online bookstores, and local bookstores. Perhaps you can find books for free at the library or at half the price at a curriculum fair. Finally, check online at www.eBay.com, www.Half.com, www.Abebooks.com, www.Alibris.com, www.TheSwap.com, www.HomeschoolClassifieds.com, and www.VegSource.com.

6. **Take expensive books on your wish list to your library director and ask what the library may be able to buy.** The director purchases books for the library regularly, based on recommendations of trade magazines and patrons like you. To ensure a better chance, narrow down your requests to those books you think others may be interested in as well as those on topics not already covered by other books in the library.

7. **When shopping, stick to your list.** You may substitute one hard-to-find or very expensive book for another on the same topic that is easier to find or less expensive, but do not buy any items that are not on your list.

Shop at stores offering teacher discounts and show proof of your homeschooling. Most stores offer teacher discounts between 10 and 20 percent to homeschoolers. Check the big bookstore chains as well as educational stores, discount stores, office supply stores, and small, locally-owned bookstores. Sometimes small bookstores give better discounts than big chains.

Resources for Free and Inexpensive Materials

You do not have to buy a packaged curriculum from a curriculum company to provide quality education for your children. Books and supplies can come from various sources. For instance, many homeschoolers go to the library as often as once a week. Through interlibrary loan, the number of available books is practically limitless, and librarians can even provide lists of grade level books. If you find an interesting book in a catalog, check it out from the library. If you decide that you want it for your home library, then buy it.

Don't forget resource libraries maintained by large churches and homeschool groups. Even when a support group does not have a library, the members often share videos and books, and a church library will likely carry Christian books not often found at the public library.

The Internet is another valuable free resource for homeschoolers. Virtual field trips save time and money. You can tour such varied places as the White House,

Mount Everest, and outer space without leaving your house. Simply search on "virtual field trips" for great destinations. Because many literary classics and primary source documents are in the public domain, complete texts and study guides are available online at such sites as www.SparkNotes.com, www.Gutenberg.net, www.FreeBookNotes.com, and www.Bartleby.com. Or simply search for the specific text, such as "Canterbury Tales online" or "text of Dante's Inferno." Also, some Web sites offer educational games, study materials, and other free resources, such as free forms and calendars at www.PrintFree.com and a free test generator at www.EasyTestMaker.com. Again, search for the specific topic or just "homeschool for free."

A number of Web sites are devoted to selling and swapping used books and supplies. Some are www.eBay.com, www.Half.com, www.Abebooks.com, www.Alibris.com, www.TheSwap.com, www.HomeschoolClassifieds.com, and www.VegSource.com. Also, many homeschool curriculum companies provide forums for their customers to sell their used materials. For a list of similar sites, search on "homeschool books for sale" or "used books."

Along with the library and Internet, a variety of other sources can provide educational provisions for free or at a low cost. Try these suggestions:

- **Borrow from friends.** They may be willing to lend you books from their home libraries.
- **Use free resources from government agencies, trade associations, and corporations.** You can get history newspapers and nature guides from your state government, art history videos from The National Gallery in Washington, D.C., as well as videos and booklets on various topics from business corporations. Go to Video Placement Worldwide at www.vpw.com and Federal Citizen Information Center at www.pueblo.gsa.gov for free videos and publications.
- **Take advantage of free community resources.** Check the yellow pages for museums, historic sites, and businesses. Peruse the newspaper for history re-enactments and festivals.
- **Add expensive items to a birthday or holiday wish list.** Relatives can give books, microscopes, and chemistry sets as gifts to your children.
- **Purchase materials at office and teacher supply stores.** You can even get an idea of what you may need, such as math manipulatives, and make them yourself at home.
- **Look for affordable workbooks at supermarkets and discount stores.** Subjects vary from pre-reading skills to multiplication.

- **Search for used items.** Used curriculum sales, yard sales, thrift stores, flea markets, Goodwill, Salvation Army, used bookstores, and the newspaper's classified section are excellent resources.

Indeed, not all homeschool supplies even have to be purchased. Some can be acquired from various sources for free. Banks and insurance companies often give away rulers, yardsticks, calculators, and calendars as promotional materials. State welcome centers, travel agencies, and chambers of commerce have maps. If you eat in restaurants that give small packs of crayons and coloring books to children of their patrons, take those crayons home with you. Contact your local newspaper and request their unused end rolls for art paper. Also, ask print shops for any scrap paper. Keep your old newspapers as drop cloths for messy art projects. Check recycling centers occasionally because schools periodically deliver old library books and textbooks for recycling; as a matter of fact, our homeschool support group began its resource library with 200 library and school books we found for free at a recycling center.

Using Open Source Software

One of the challenges facing today's homeschooling families is the cost of technology. Most traditional students have access to school computer labs, but for homeschoolers, this option can add additional expenses that may be overwhelming. Have you seen the price for a good word processor or spreadsheet system lately? However, thanks to the foresight and wisdom of different leaders in the computer science environment, there are alternatives: The Free Software and Open Source Movements.

Open Source software, as defined by the Open Source Definition, is software under a license that permits free distribution, includes source code, and permits creation of derivative works. For more information, go to www.GNU.org and www.OpenSource.org.

As a result of the Free Software and Open Source Movements, thousands of free, quality software packages are available on the Internet. All you have to do is download them. They work with all major operating systems, including Windows, Mac OSX, Linux, and BSD. Here are some of the best that you can use in your home:

- **OpenOffice is a package featuring a word processor, spreadsheet, multimedia presentation manager, and drawing program.** As a matter of fact, this book has been written using OpenOffice. Go to www.OpenOffice.org to download. If you download only this one, it will more than pay for the cost of this book. For free tutorials, go to www.TutorialsForOpenOffice.org and www.OpenOfficeSupport.com/tutorials.html.

- **Thunderbird is a SPAM-blocking email reader.** Go to www.Mozilla.org to download.
- **FireFox is a virus-resilient, pop-up blocking Web browser.** Go to www.Mozilla.org to download.
- **School Forge offers education-related and school-related software.** This includes grade tracking and educational software for classes. Go to www.SchoolForge.net to download.

If you use Open Source software, your home computer can mimic the functions of computers in the best private and public schools as well as in many businesses. Best of all, you will have done it for free!

Creative Ways to Pay for Supplies

If your family is on a budget, you can always purchase curriculum materials a little at a time rather than all at once. Your curriculum will be a lot more affordable if the cost is spread over several months rather than paid in one lump sum. Similarly, some families put a certain amount of their monthly income as "educational expenses" into a savings account and actually treat it as a monthly bill. By setting aside a certain amount each month, they do not have to worry about available money for books or swimming lessons or field trips to the museum. Alternatively, many families set aside a portion of their tax refund into a homeschool fund.

On the other hand, many homeschoolers simply find creative ways to make money to purchase the supplies they want. These suggestions may help you:

- **Start a small home-based business.** Not only will it provide you with extra money to purchase school necessities, it will also teach your children about small business.
- **Get a seasonal or temporary job.** You could sign up with a temporary employment agency, work for a package delivery company during holidays, and deliver the annual phone books.
- **Use birthday and Christmas money given by extended relatives.** Allocate part of the money for homeschool expenses and use the rest for fun items.
- **Sell used books online or at curriculum fairs.** Use the money to buy materials for next year.

- **Organize an annual yard sale.** Offer to undertake a friend's yard sale for a small percentage.
- **Be thrifty in other budgeted areas.** If you spend a little time planning meals, cutting coupons, and comparing prices, you could put the grocery money you save each week into your homeschool fund. Similarly, if you purchase clothes on sale, put the remaining amount of money allocated for clothes into your homeschool fund.

Ways To Cut Expenses

In addition to finding creative ways to make money, many families find resourceful ways to cut expenses so they can afford the curricula they want for their children. A very important element to cutting expenses is establishing a home budget. Many families use financial planning systems to help them live within their means and pay off debts, which translate into available funds for homeschool supplies.

You may find that cutting back on entertainment expenses will make a difference. For example, rent movies rather than go to the cinema, go on picnics rather than out to expensive restaurants, or spend the day at the YMCA pool rather than go to the beach for the weekend. Schedule day trips to local areas. Some families vacation at home by setting aside a weekend, turning off the phone, and planning fun foods and activities together as a family. Others camp out in the backyard. The resulting extra money is channeled into the homeschool fund.

Here are additional ways that other families save money at home:

- **Purchase clothes on sale and accept hand-me-downs.** Also, pack up your children's outgrown clothes to use for each subsequent child.
- **Buy groceries in bulk.** Stock up on meat and other high-priced items when on sale.
- **Combine errands to conserve gas.** This saves time as well as wear and tear on your car.
- **Buy used cars, furniture and computers.** You may even be able to barter for some of them.
- **Do things yourself when possible.** Change the oil in the cars, trim the children's hair, mow the lawn, and sew your own clothes to stretch your budget. You may even be able to do simple home repairs from a do-it-yourself manual from *Reader's Digest*.

These are just a few practical ideas. You can find even more suggestions from Web sites and books on frugal living and large families that will help you save money at home. Check out www.LoveAtHome.com, www.FrugalFamilyNetwork.com, and www.FrugalLiving.About.com for great ideas, and use the money you save to meet your children's educational needs.

Chapter 5

Storage and Supplies: What You Need and What You Can Get by Without

Organize your homeschool supplies in one area to make them easy to access and put away.

You do not need an elaborate setup to homeschool. Expensive science equipment and even school desks are not necessary. Buy supplies as you need them, make your own manipulatives, use your dining room table for school, and store your materials in a hall closet. Of course, some supplies may be convenient to have on hand, and a few are absolute necessities.

Supply Checklists

Depending on the ages of your children, consider stocking these school supplies.

Some of these things you will definitely need to start:
- Pencils, pens, erasers, highlighters, pencil sharpener
- Lined writing paper, notebook paper, drawing paper, construction paper
- Binders, spiral notebooks
- Craft supplies (crayons, markers, paint, scissors, glue, construction paper, poster board)
- Math manipulatives (beans, beads, Popsicle sticks, etc.)
- Library card

Some of these you may need:
- Flashcards of the alphabet, numbers, mathematics
- Magnetic numbers and letters
- Ruler, protractor, compass, calculator
- Globe or world map
- Sports equipment
- Miscellaneous craft supplies (empty cans, paper towel rolls, old socks, etc.)
- Index cards, graph paper
- Educational games, jigsaw puzzles, magnifying glass, magnet set
- Analog clock
- Dictionary, thesaurus, encyclopedias
- Dry erase board or chalk board

Some of these things you will need for organization:
- Wall or pocket calendar
- Storage containers (boxes, milk crates, baskets)
- File folders
- Bookshelves

Some of these you may want at some point:
- Computer
- Printer

- Internet access
- Educational software
- Lap desks
- Answering machine
- Copier

Keep a large stock on hand, namely hundreds of pencils and dozens of packs of notebook paper, to prevent wasted time searching for lost pencils or running out to buy paper. Buy these items in bulk during clearance sales after the back-to-school rush! Keep an on-going list of items that need replenishing. Take the list with you to the store to remind you of your needs and to keep you from buying unnecessary things and blowing your budget.

With more than one child to homeschool, you need to take good care of the resources you have. Store reusable materials when not in use and save them for younger students. One mother in our homeschool group takes workbooks apart, puts each page in a clear page protector, and places all the pages in a binder. With washable markers, the pages can be used over and over.

Storing Supplies

Keep supplies in one area to make them easy to access and put away. Perhaps turn a hall closet into a homeschool supply closet. Line it with shelves, or put an old dresser in the closet and fill the space above it with shelves. Similarly, you could add a bookcase and filing cabinet to one corner of your dining room, or you could use the bottom of a china cabinet or kitchen cupboard. Our family has used these locations at various times over the years. In tight quarters, store supplies in flat boxes under sofas and beds. Having a central location saves wasted time searching for necessary items; plus, you will know at a glance when to restock.

Wherever you store your supplies, put some fun learning materials in a place where children can reach them easily when you are helping another child or when they are just in the mood to play with them. Include blocks, puzzles, books, magnets, and craft supplies. You will be encouraged by how often your children turn to these for recreation.

Storing Books

Place current books, workbooks, notebooks, and other shared materials on a convenient shelf or in a basket in the room where your family does the majority of shared subjects. We keep a large basket in the dining room for this purpose.

Having books conveniently nearby saves time as each student moves from subject to subject. The books to be used later in the year are kept on a specific shelf in the supply area until needed.

Set aside an area for your home library and start collecting books as soon as possible. Select classics that will be read over and over with each subsequent child. Since this one-time investment will be used by all your children at some point, these books will be well worth the money you spend on them. Also, since you will be accumulating a lot of books, build or purchase several bookshelves to start and plan to add more later.

You may want to devote a shelf to library books so they will not get mixed up with your home collection or get lost in the house. Perhaps keep them in a canvas tote bag. We keep our library books in a basket in the den, and we have a rule that all library books must be returned to this location. A central spot makes them easy to gather up when heading for the library.

Finally, set aside space on high shelves or in storage bins for future curricula, whether new books you order for next year or used books you want to save for the next child. As you order materials, not only will you be able to make sure everything arrives, but also even your most destructive children will be unable to damage or lose anything before you need it.

Keep these long-term books and materials on shelves or in bins divided by subject or grade level. Some families divide supplies by grade; they keep all third grade materials together, all fourth grade together, etc. Other families group subjects, such as all science resources together, all history together, and then label the book spines with the appropriate grade levels. Follow the method that works best for your family.

If a small living space forces you to store materials at the end of each year, let your children choose the books they want to keep out, and pack up the others. Use clear storage bins so you can easily see what is inside, or clearly label them by grade, and stack them in the attic or basement. Use flat boxes for easy storage under sofas and beds. Some families intentionally store books until they are needed again even though they have plenty of space to keep them all out. This way their children will not have read them in a couple of years and they will be "fresh."

Displaying and Storing Artwork and Projects

With all your kids' artwork, crafts, models, and science projects, you will quickly run out of room for display and storage. Time to get creative before your refrigerator gets covered! Create a gallery for your artists. String clothesline or yarn along a wall of the family room or hallway and use clothespins to hang the pictures. Purchase inexpensive frames and hang up your favorites. As you rotate out the old ones, date and save a representative sample in a box, and throw away the others.

If you have difficulty throwing anything away, find creative alternatives for the leftover masterpieces. Here are some ideas:

- **Laminate them to make placemats.** Your kids will like seeing their artwork under their plates.
- **Recycle them as book covers, gift wrap, and cards.** Each one of our children selects a picture to include in birthday cards and gifts that we mail to relatives.
- **Color-copy the artwork for other projects.** One family in our homeschool group uses them in scrapbooks and calendars.
- **Scan the artwork and store them on CDs.** Later you can always print them, email them to friends or make cards out of them.

For a science project or three-dimensional model, display it for a while and take a picture of it. Include your child in the photo, too. Then place the labeled photo in a portfolio, scrapbook or family photo album. With a photographic record, you no longer have to store the original, so you can discard it to make room for new constructions.

The Work Area

Now you need a place for creating those projects and doing school work. Some families are lucky enough to turn a spare room or basement into a classroom, with desks, wall space for displaying artwork, a chalk board or dry erase board, a computer, and a large table for projects. A separate place for school is convenient when you have to stop working in the middle of a project; you can leave it and pick up where you left off later. That may be rather difficult if the school table doubles as the dinner table.

However, you do not need a school room to homeschool successfully. Most families do just fine around the dining room table or at the kitchen counter. They gather on the sofa or spread out on the living room floor. If your children work better separate from each other, put desks in their bedrooms or give them lap desks. Just make sure their work areas have adequate lighting.

Make the most of whatever space you have, whether a spare room, guest room, basement or dining room. Make it comfortable for you and your kids, and it will work out fine. What the room looks like is not important; it is what you do in it that matters. Just like any other part of your house, as you live in your designated school room you will rearrange it over time to fit your changing needs.

Files and Notebooks

To prevent the work area from becoming overcrowded with books, workbooks, and notebooks, give each child a book bag or container to hold his or her own daily materials. This also gives each child the responsibility for keeping up with his own belongings.

While each child should keep his own books, you need to keep files for each child. Allot separate files for each one to keep track of progress and to use for a future portfolio, if necessary. Also, keep a file on any paperwork and correspondence related to school officials.

Generally, after the first day, your students will never be in the same week for every subject. If your curriculum provides instructor's manuals or guides, use sticky notes to keep track of where you are in each subject. Section the manual by coloring the outside edge of pages with different highlighters or by using colored dividers so you can quickly find the section you need. Do the same to organize your children's notebooks.

If you design your own lesson plans, create an idea file for each subject on paper or in your word processor. Browse through reference books for ideas, write them down, and place them in the idea file for the appropriate subject. As you research information and activities on magnets, for example, you will likely come across ideas for other topics. When you do, note the book and page numbers or Web site addresses and place them in your idea file. Later, when you research the next topic, you will already have a head start.

Similar to the idea file is a notebook or binder to organize your ideas and paperwork. Place any kind of documentation in it, from your own notes to field trip brochures. Take a picture of the science model that took up half of your kitchen counter and put it in the notebook, too. You can also include interesting articles that you read. Keep a spiral notebook by your bed to journal daily activities each night, and add the full notebook to the binder. If you are uncertain about saving something, put it in the binder just in case. About three or four times a year, go through and discard items you no longer need. At the end of the year, label and save the notebook to serve as a record of all your family did that year.

Containers

In addition to notebooks and files, sort materials in labeled containers. You do not have to buy name brand containers; just recycle empty shoe boxes, coffee tins, oatmeal containers, baby wipe containers, peanut butter jars and butter dishes. Use zipper food storage bags for manipulatives, game pieces, puzzle pieces, cutouts and pencils. Keep a separate large container for frequently used supplies such as paper, pencils and erasers.

Use large plastic bins or crates to hold each child's current workbooks, notebooks, artwork, and projects. At the end of the year, transfer them to large folders or envelopes for storage so you can reuse the containers next year. Write the grade level on the folders and store them in separate office boxes or plastic bins, one for each child.

Color-Coding

As a homeschooling parent of more than one child, you will find color-coding to be a valuable organizational tool. Using colors is easy. Purchase colored felt-tip markers, add color to computer-generated labels or buy colored stickers. Use them to color-code files, organizers, and storage crates by subject, activity, or grade. Add colored stickers to the spines of books to designate reading level. Then you can shelve them by subject and still be able to pull out the grade level you need at a glance.

When you assign colors to your children, use those colors for everything. Each child should have his own plastic bin, book bag, three-ring binder, spiral notebooks, pencils, and pencil sharpener, all of one color. Not only will this eliminate misunderstandings when something is left out, but also you will know which bin to look in to find a specific child's work.

Home Computer

Although a home computer is not necessary, it will be helpful in many ways. Computer programs ease record-keeping. Even if you never utilize a program specifically designed for homeschoolers, you can use a spreadsheet to track grades and a word processor to keep book lists. Free Internet lesson plans and virtual field trips help keep homeschool costs down. Plus, commercial software and games as well as free online applications reinforce concepts in your students' lessons. Under your supervision, they can also use the Internet to learn research skills.

Indeed, they will need to learn how to use a computer eventually as nearly all fields of study and careers use computers to some degree. However, don't feel you are depriving your children if you do not have a computer. They can always use computers at the library, neighbor's house or grandparents' home.

Chapter 6

Secrets of the One-Room Schoolhouse

When you read aloud, be sure all your children can gather around you to see the pictures or just be near you.

Like the school teacher of the one-room schoolhouse era, you face some of the same challenges as you teach several subjects to students of different ages. While you may not care to duplicate the uncomfortable desks and the hours-long school day, you may want to take advantage of certain benefits and apply various principles associated with that by-gone era. Many of today's veteran homeschoolers of multiple children have discovered these methods through experience, trial, and error. Consider these suggestions to make the most of schooling multiple students.

Sharing Subjects

For the most efficient use of your teaching time, share subjects across grade levels as much as possible. Our two oldest daughters have always shared Bible, history, and science. Once our son and youngest daughter were old enough, they joined them, and they all started learning Spanish together. If your children are within a few grades of each other, they can share such subjects easily.

While sharing subjects, all your children will study the same historical period or the same science topic at the same time, but on their own learning levels. You may even be able to use the same book for all of them; simply read the text aloud to everyone and explain difficult concepts to younger children as you go along. Then assign individual work to each child.

It is important, however, for assignments, additional books, and hands-on activities to be based on the individual abilities and interests of each child. That way, each child will learn at his own level and will not compare his abilities to an older sibling's abilities. Even if you are careful not to compare, your children will likely do so. After all, you understand that an older child should be better and faster at reading, narrating, writing essays, and multiplying than younger children, but younger children may not understand and may feel inadequate in comparison. Alternatively, a younger child may excel in a subject that an older child struggles with, such as spelling. Having his younger sibling constantly doing better may harm your older child's self-esteem. To avoid this problem, assign separate work and keep their unique perspectives in mind. If sharing seems to have a detrimental effect, stop doing it.

To share subjects successfully, use the grade level of the oldest child or a grade level between children. If you teach from a level above your oldest child, you will have to explain concepts to everyone nearly all the time. Similarly, if you use a book below the level of everyone, you will have to assign extra work to each child to make the subject challenging enough. For a balance between assigning extra work to older students and explaining difficult concepts to younger students, use the grade level of the oldest child or between the children.

Another option is to start simple and dismiss students when the lesson gets too difficult for them. Anita does this with her four children. For example, read aloud to all the children from the third grader's history book. Then give your third grader a break while you do more in-depth study with his older siblings on the same topic. This allows your older children to learn the lesson in a broad context first and in more detail later.

If your students do not enjoy being read to, let them read the assignments on their own. Some students could still share the same books. On the other hand, you may want to use different grade level books and have them discuss together what they have read to gain different perspectives on the same topic.

Here are additional tips to make sharing subjects easier:

- **Set aside adequate space to accommodate everyone.** If you read aloud on the sofa, be sure all your children can gather around you to see the pictures or just be near you. Similarly, place the computer where several children can view it at once when necessary.
- **Establish beforehand if students are allowed to call out answers or if they must raise their hands when you ask a question.** Otherwise, you may end up with a rowdy group or one child who monopolizes all the questions.
- **Stagger their schedules.** If three children need the computer for a typing lesson program, schedule their lessons so that all three are not ready to use the computer at the same time.
- **Choose a topic that the majority of those sharing the subject want to learn.** For example, if two children want to learn about plants while only one is interested in dinosaurs, go with plants first. Promise to make dinosaurs the next focus.
- **Pick a convenient time for everyone.** Our family shares lessons in the morning and reserves afternoons for individual work, but do what is convenient for your family.
- **Assign individual reports and projects to be shared with everyone.** For example, if the group studies the Middle Ages, assign further research on castles to one child, knights and armor to another child, clothing to one child, and illnesses and medicine to another child. Then the end product, whether a report, story, drama, puppet show, model, or poster, will be shared with the group so that everyone learns from each student's research.

For subjects impossible to share, such as math, you can make matters easier by having everyone work on the same subject at the same time in the same location. Although students are working from different books, you will be available to help as needed and will be able to ensure that they all get their work done.

The Option to Skip Grades

Another option when sharing subjects is to advance one child a grade or two so that two children will be studying on the same grade level. Some subjects are repetitive; math and grammar are two examples. If next year's math book covers the same concepts as this past year's book and the concepts are not that much more advanced, consider promoting one child to the next grade level so you will have two at the same level. This works particularly well when one student excels at a subject. After all, one of the benefits of homeschooling is the ability to tailor each child's education to meet his skill level rather than his age.

However, make such a decision based on the student's academic ability, not on saving instruction time. You do not want an older student bored by easy material; nor do you want a younger child working at a level that is too challenging or comparing his abilities unfavorably to his older sibling's abilities. Do not sacrifice a child's self-esteem just to save instruction time in group lessons.

Keeping Their Attention

Keeping your students' attention during group lessons and making sure they are "getting it" may sometimes be difficult, especially if you are reading aloud to students who are not auditory learners. Older students may listen better if they take notes. Give younger children an activity to keep them busy. One child may listen best while lying on the floor, tossing a ball up in the air and catching it. Another child may color or crochet. While I read aloud, my eight-year-old son bounces on a large exercise ball, providing just enough activity for him to focus on listening.

Here are a few suggestions to help you manage a group of students and to make sure all of them are listening and understanding the material:

- **Ask them to recap everything they remember before you start reading each day.** Recapping where you left off is a great introduction to reading what happens next.
- **Take turns having each child read small portions aloud.** This will also improve their reading skills.
- **Ask questions about what has just been read every few sentences or paragraphs.** Knowing they will be questioned may get them to pay attention. When they answer incorrectly, repeat the information and ask again. Reward first-time correct answers with verbal praise, a nickel, small candy or another tiny treat.
- **Act out scenes from history.** Change your voice for different characters or have an impromptu drama scene where each child portrays a different person.
- **Use the narration method.** After reading, have students write five things they remember, or ask them to write everything they remember within a

five-minute time period. Pre-writers can draw a picture. You can even title, date, and collect the daily sheets for their notebooks.

Scheduling One-on-One Instruction

For students whose ages prevent them from sharing subjects, such as a tenth grader, sixth grader, third grader, and preschooler, you must schedule your day a little more. As Pam does with her daughters, set aside a certain time for each child. To ensure that this works smoothly with several students, give each one a to-do list or set up a chart in a central location. At the beginning of the day, make sure that each child understands what to do that day and how to do his first lesson. Then start with the youngest and progress to the oldest. While you work with one, the others can work on independent assignments. Then switch to the next student.

Sometimes one student may need more attention on reading or math, for example. Anita, a homeschooling mom of four, routinely finds a quiet spot in the house or outside somewhere to read a book together or do algebra. She takes that child on errands with her, so they can work on spelling or multiplication in the car together. She also uses her cooking time to give extra help. The child sits at the counter and reads aloud or studies while Anita cooks.

Even if your children are not close enough in age to teach them the same material at the same time, perhaps they may be far enough apart not to be in high school at the same time. This has been the case with Pam's children, and she considers it a benefit because it allows her to focus on a comprehensive college prep curriculum for one student at a time.

Independent Study

As a homeschooling parent of more than one child, you need students who can study independently while you devote one-on-one instruction with another student. At the beginning of the school year, decide which subjects each child can do independently and explain what they are. If a child understands the instructions, he should be able to work on his own. You do not need to sit right beside him, but you may need to remain in the same room or in the next room working with another child or doing a household chore. That way you can monitor any restlessness and be available for help. If students prefer studying in their own rooms, be sure to check on their progress periodically to eliminate potential problems and prevent wasted time. If you think that you may get distracted and forget to check on them, set a timer to remind you.

To encourage independent study, label the front of an index card with each subject. On the back, write the total amount of time to be spent on that subject for the day and list in order what should be done in that subject. Perhaps add a fun activity at the end for any spare minutes, such as computer time or another pastime your child enjoys.

Another method is to use a timer and start with short assignments. Gradually increase the size of the assignments and the length of time as your child's skills and confidence improve. This method also works well for teaching students to stay focused on a task.

Keeping Each Child Focused

If your children are to work independently, they need to be disciplined enough to stay focused on a task. Staying focused on an assignment, even when boring, is a learned condition. Some children can develop serious time management problems if they are not taught early on to discipline themselves to complete an "unfavorite" task in a reasonable length of time. It can take years to correct this, so start early with your children. Help them to discipline themselves by encouraging them to finish what they set out to do.

When our own children were preschoolers, we would use inexpensive workbooks so they could "do school." I would assign one page with about five problems. Once completed, they would nearly always ask for another page. This would continue for several pages. Eventually, they would get tired in the middle of a page. Rather than let them quit, I would insist that they complete the page. They had asked to do it, so they had to finish before they could quit. This not only trained them to finish their work but also increased their attention span a little at a time. Now that they are older and must finish a math assignment, for example, they are able to stay focused and complete the task in a reasonable amount of time.

An older student who cannot stay focused is not beyond your help now. Again, start with short assignments and gradually increase them. For example, set a time limit for a fairly short math, grammar, or spelling assignment. Place your student in a quiet place, but not too far from you. Each day add to the time and assignment until she can work about an hour on her own.

Here are a few more tips to keep your students focused on the task at hand:

- **Remove distractions.** Have a quiet place for each student to study, away from games, toys, and television. Remind children to use "inside" voices so they will not disrupt students.

- **Teach the easily distracted child first.** Have the others work on individual assignments.
- **Schedule difficult or boring subjects when your children are most alert.** Usually, this would be in the morning. Then during the afternoon, when most children are tired and easily distracted, they can work on projects or subjects that they enjoy.
- **Avoid busy work.** If your child understands the work, let him move on to the next lesson.
- **Prepare a detailed to-do list.** For example, my son gets distracted easily with verbal instructions. On the other hand, he stays focused if he has a list that specifies to clean up from breakfast, brush his teeth, do handwriting, do three pages of phonics, etc. Plus, knowing he will be done at a certain point motivates him to work diligently.
- **Assign leftover work as homework.** Set a timer for a reasonable period, and any work not completed is "homework" that has to be done during playtime. A few days of doing school work during free time will inspire your students to stay focused during school time.
- **Praise your child when he has stayed focused on an assignment.** Praise is a good incentive to get him to do it again!

Sometimes active children stay focused on a subject better if they are moving while studying. They bounce a ball while reviewing the multiplication tables and skip rope while spelling words. Similarly, my oldest daughter is more productive when listening to music while doing algebra.

Occasionally, you yourself may be unable to keep from yawning! Start the morning with a quick shower. If your mind wanders while you are listening to a child read aloud, drink a cup of coffee or a glass of ice water to perk you up. Make sure you are getting plenty of sleep. In fact, make sure all of you get plenty of sleep and eat well-balanced meals. Plan little nutritious snacks throughout the day to keep your energy levels up and to help you all stay focused.

Managing Interruptions

Interruptions cause students to lose focus. Prevent unnecessary interruptions by reviewing with your children what constitutes an emergency and explaining what to do when they need your help with school work while you are busy with another child. This not only prevents frequent interruptions during one-on-one time, but also saves wasted time waiting on you. Although you will be unable to get to every child's need as soon as he requests it, learning to wait will teach patience.

While waiting their turn with you, students can do the following:

- Mark the difficult question and continue on to the next one.
- Start another subject or work on an ongoing project.
- Access a shelf or drawer of puzzles, arts and crafts supplies, magnet sets or books.
- Do a quick household chore.
- Ask an older sibling for help.

How Older Children Can Help

Enlist the help of your older students in certain subjects. They can read history, Bible, and literature assignments to younger siblings. This gives them more practice reading aloud and gives you time to spend with another child or on housework. Promote the oldest student to teaching assistant and have her teach a group subject, such as science. As a result, she learns the material well enough to teach it to lower levels; plus, it means less work for you!

Ask an older child who loves to read to listen to a younger sibling read. Ask an older daughter who loves math to help her little brother with his math. She can explain the instructions, go over sample problems, be available for help, and check his work. Not only are you free to work with another child, but also your older daughter gets a chance to get closer to her brother, reinforce early math concepts, and increase her self-confidence.

Regardless of age, ask those who are skilled in a particular subject to help others who are not as good. This is an opportunity to encourage your children use their talents to help others.

Children love to teach younger children and "play" school, but you may be surprised how much they actually learn. Indeed, I never taught my three younger children the alphabet, numbers, and colors; they learned from their older sister while playing school.

How Family and Friends Can Help

You do not have to be the sole teacher. Even if your husband works full time, he could read literature aloud at bedtime, correct school work daily or weekly, and teach a subject that he knows better than you do in the evenings or on weekends. Perhaps he could handle extracurricular activities, such as scouts, clubs, and sports.

If possible, your husband may be able to telecommute from home or cut back his full time job. This has allowed Victoria's husband to have time to teach French and science to their seven children as well as oversee the family's construction of a guest house. In our own family, we have been most productive and closest as a family when my husband worked at home.

Ask a friend or relative to teach a subject once a week. Your uncle may be a math whiz, so he can teach calculus. Your sister may have majored in English in college, so she can grade essays.

You could also share a subject with another homeschooling family. One parent teaches the lesson one week and the other parent teaches the next week. You would be co-oping a class, but with fewer children involved.

Handling Multiple Learning Styles

You have probably read or heard about "learning styles." Learning styles are simply different ways of learning. Of course, your child will learn no matter what style you use, but the best style will be the one that is most productive for him. You need to discover how each child learns best and use that information to teach him.

Generally, people fall into three categories. Auditory learners prefer to learn by discussing and listening to someone talk about the information. Visual learners would rather read or see a demonstration, and kinesthetic learners favor hands-on applications. Schools use all these methods in various ways, but as a homeschooling parent you can focus on the one that fits each child's needs best.

The difficulty occurs when your children exhibit a variety of learning styles. Plus, you may have a different learning style yourself, and generally you will teach best using your own style. This works out great for students who learn the same way you do, but not so well for those who have a different style. As a result, some parents opt to teach what works for them. After all, they need to be comfortable teaching, and they may become overwhelmed by trying to adapt to multiple learning styles. Although this means that one or two of their children must fit into their parents' styles to some extent, parents can still utilize other learning styles occasionally.

In your case, visual learners could watch a video or look at pictures related to the topic or even read the books on their own while you read them aloud to the auditory learners. Kinesthetic learners could draw a picture or color while you read aloud. Additionally, they could act out what you have read for the auditory and visual learners. Experiment with different arrangements and see what works best for each child.

Numerous books and Web sites explain how to determine learning styles and multiple intelligences and how to implement those styles in your teaching. Ask your librarian or search the Internet for more information.

Chapter 7

Plans and Schedules: Making the Most of Your Time

*When your children have their own to-do lists, they can
work at their own pace and feel some control over their day.*

Don't worry that planning and scheduling will stifle creativity and spontaneity or make every day mundane and routine. Actually, organization will get routine tasks out of the way, making you more productive, giving you precious time with each child, and providing extra time overall for creative and spontaneous activities. The more prepared you are, the less likely you will waste valuable time.

Advance Preparation

Be sure to order your books far enough in advance so that you will receive them in time, whether you order a complete curriculum all at once, stagger your orders from various companies throughout the year, or take advantage of interlibrary loan. Take into account time delays in deliveries due to holidays as well as any seasonal constraints the company may face. During late summer and fall, when curriculum companies may be overwhelmed by orders, your materials may take eight weeks or more to arrive, and some items may be on backorder. Therefore, order in the spring if possible.

When new materials come in, go through them to ensure everything you ordered has arrived. Get the teacher's manuals or instructor's guides organized and ready to use. Take time to skim through each book and workbook. Decide how they may be adapted to your children, what sections you may need to skip, and how each book may be divided to accommodate your school year. Then store everything in the appropriate place until needed. Some families place materials on bookshelves right away, while others store them in plastic bins until needed.

If you use the library, ask how long you can place a book on hold and how long it takes to receive a book on interlibrary loan. Also, find out how long you can keep a book checked out, how many books you can check out at one time, and how many times you can renew the books. Keep the answers in mind when planning to use library books during the year.

Sample Yearly Schedules

Your yearly schedule can be as flexible as necessary as long as you meet the required number of days for your state. Many homeschoolers start off following the public school calendar and do school Monday through Friday, September through May. They take the usual school holidays and use summer months to plan for the coming academic year.

That is how our family started off as well. We had completed our first year of home education by the time our third child was born, and we were taking three months off as our summer vacation. However, after only two weeks, our kindergartener and preschooler wanted to do school and asked why we had not done it in so long. After consideration, I decided that a year-round schedule would, indeed, work best for us. Such a flexible arrangement would give us three or four school days per week, leaving extra time for our playgroup, field trips, and long holiday breaks. We would also avoid the lengthy summer break that usually necessitates three to four weeks of extensive review in the fall. Ever since then we have homeschooled year-round, using the last couple of months of our school calendar to plan for next year.

You, too, can create a yearly schedule that fits your unique family. Any plan will work as long as you consistently follow it. Here are other schedules that you may use:

- **Alternate weeks of school with weeks off.** Schedule three weeks of school and one week off, or four weeks of school and one week off, or six weeks of school and two weeks off. Coordinate the weeks off with holidays so everyone can look forward to regular breaks.
- **School for three months followed by one full month off.** Schedule school during September, October, and November, with December off; school during January, February, and March, with April off; and school during May, June, and July, with August off. Each month off can be used to prepare for the next three months.
- **Divide the school year into quarters.** Schedule school for ten straight weeks followed by two-week breaks. This will leave you with four extra weeks to use as needed.
- **Spend the traditional months doing traditional subjects.** Use the summer months for fun activities, such as swimming lessons, music, art, math games, pleasure reading, educational movies, vacations and outings.

Planning Your Own Yearly Schedule

You will save so much time and energy by planning your year in advance. Of course, write in pencil because you may need to make changes from month to month or week to week as you implement your schedule. Making periodic changes to a tentative schedule will be much easier than jumping into the school year with no plan at all.

Before scheduling anything, however, you need an idea of the number of days in your school year. First, find out the number of days required by your state. Then purchase a pocket or wall calendar, or print a calendar from the Internet. We use the calendars at www.PrintFree.com, but a variety of calendars are available online. Simply search on "free printable calendar."

With the total number of necessary school days in mind, begin by marking out summer breaks, holidays, and family vacations. Allot extra days off for a few long weekends, sick days, and a day here and there to enjoy the cool autumn or warm spring weather. If you end up not needing those days, then you will have extra time either at the end of your school year or to spread out among your remaining holidays and breaks.

Be sure to pre-plan church and family events, such as trips to and visits from relatives, and extracurricular activities, such as piano lessons and scouts. Set aside days for running errands, visiting the library, and going to doctor and dental appointments. Teenagers, especially, will have their own schedules that you need to consider when planning the family schedule. If you do not plan ahead, you will likely run into unexpected scheduling conflicts at the last minute.

If you use a boxed curriculum, simply follow the lesson plans that come with it and pencil them onto your calendar. You may need to make adjustments, such as doubling up a few days in certain subjects and doing others every other day. You can follow the curriculum's schedule closely or more loosely, depending on your homeschooling style. For example, during the years in which we use a packaged curriculum with a 36-week schedule, I determine the halfway point on the calendar so I will know to be done with week 18 about that time. I also figure out approximately where the quarter marks are in the year. Periodically referring to this schedule ensures that we stay relatively on track. Other homeschoolers, such as Victoria's family of seven children, work on the curriculum until they finish, or resume in the fall where they left off the previous spring.

If you order a mix of materials, you can easily determine a schedule on your own. Simply divide the number of pages by the number of school days. The result is the number of pages that must be covered each school day. Divide lessons and chapters the same way.

Sample Weekly and Daily Schedules

Follow the lesson plans designed by the curriculum company you use, or modify them to fit your family or to suit each child. No schedule is typical, so find a routine that matches your unique family. Here are some schedules that work for other families:

- **Use the 25/5 schedule.** The plan is to work on a subject for 25 minutes, take a five-minute break, and then work on the next subject. No matter how many pages are completed, work stops after 25 minutes. The next day your student picks up where he left off. Some families extend the working time for older children and reduce the time for younger children.
- **Give a choice.** For example, tell your child to read 15 pages or one chapter, whichever is shortest.
- **Follow a typical college schedule.** Mondays and Wednesdays could be devoted to history and language arts, and Tuesdays and Thursdays to math

and science. Your children do one week's worth of work on those two days. Reserve Fridays for special projects, field trips, free time or make-up work.

- **Block out subjects.** Instead of doing language arts every day, do phonics and spelling one day, grammar and vocabulary the next day. You do not have to do every subject every day.
- **Differentiate between morning and afternoon.** Devote morning hours to the basics, such as language arts, math, and science. Set aside afternoons for reading and working on projects.
- **Allow each child to choose from a list of assignments.** Sometimes one student may spend an entire week on one subject. However, the following week he will probably catch up on other subjects. This method works well if a child has difficulty transitioning between subjects or prefers finishing a project or book before moving on to something else.

Scheduling Your Week

Plan to devote about an hour over the weekend to prepare for the upcoming week. This advance preparation will make each day much more productive. Look over the assignments for the week, and make any changes you feel are necessary to adapt the curriculum to your individual children. Remember, you do not have to follow the lesson plan of a packaged curriculum to the letter if you would like to do something different.

Then, note what you need for that week's activities and projects, see how many supplies you already have, and make a list of items to purchase. One mom in our homeschool group delegates the job of project coordinator to her oldest child, who lists the necessary materials and searches the house for them. Then mom takes her shopping for the remaining items. If you do this, make a big deal out of the project coordinator position, so your child will feel important and appreciated. Perhaps let the position rotate among your oldest children.

Once you have assignments and supplies under control, add errands, grocery shopping, and extracurricular activities. As a homeschooling parent of more than one child, you will likely finish with a full week of school, activities, and errands, so you need this schedule to keep from forgetting anything.

Scheduling Your Day

Some parents get up in the morning before their kids do to prepare for the day. Others spend about 30 minutes the night before each day. In either case, make a list in order of what has to be done. You can use a lesson plan book, a dry erase board or an index card posted on the refrigerator. Then just work down the list.

Some families try to duplicate school at home and schedule an hour for each subject five days a week. While this plan may work very well with one or two children, if you have more, you risk frustration and burnout. Besides, why would you want to duplicate school at home? A homeschooler does not need the same amount of time as a classroom of students needs to accomplish the same amount of work. As a homeschooling parent, you can stop explaining the material as soon as each child understands. You will know from your observations and discussions whether he understands or not, so he does not have to do all the problems on a page. Give him practice, and when he masters the material, move on. Similarly, when he does not understand, you have the freedom to spend more time explaining and to give him more practice until he does understand.

With this in mind, do not set up a rigid daily timetable where every minute is planned; instead, prepare a general schedule just to set up a routine. Write in pencil because the unexpected will interrupt your schedule occasionally. When it does, don't freak out; simply turn those unexpected events into "teachable moments" when possible, and return to your original schedule when you can. Similarly, if your kids are really into a project, don't stop them just to stay on schedule. Remember, a schedule is there to help you, not restrict you.

Perhaps your family does not work well on a schedule, even a flexible one. After all, unschoolers homeschool successfully without scheduled academics. In that case, devise a simple routine in order to allow time for chores, errands, reading, extracurricular activities, and projects. Perhaps write down the goals for the week, but don't specify which day to do them. Sometimes your students may do only one subject on one day, then four subjects the next day. In any case, you will be structured enough to meet your goals, but in a more flexible and relaxed way. If you write in pencil, you will ensure even more flexibility for last-minute ideas.

Schedules and To-Do Lists for Students

For very large families, divide your children into age groups. For example, our two older daughters share subjects together, and our younger son and daughter share subjects. You may need to schedule more one-on-one time with the younger group and use informal time to discuss books, current events, and other issues with your high school group. Actually, your high school students should be able to arrange their own schedules with only slight guidance from you, if any. Depending on how independent you have trained your children to be, your middle school and junior high school students may be able to schedule their days on their own as well.

Train even your youngest students to be responsible for completing their school work. As part of your preparation each day, list all the school work each child needs to do in pencil on an index card or notebook paper. Then organize subjects that are done on alternating days. For example, divide language arts into grammar and spelling on one day and creative writing and vocabulary on the next day. Then rearrange each child's list so that each one will be doing individual work while you are working one-on-one with another child.

If your children work best with a detailed to-do list, then include chores, lunch, free time, and piano practice, for example. Alternate academics with quick chores and fun pursuits. Also, include activities to choose from when they have to wait for you, such as puzzles, computer games, special projects, or light chores. Letting each child choose an activity works much better than telling him to wait a moment or go play until you are available for one-on-one instruction with him.

Each morning, give each child his own to-do list or post a master list on the refrigerator color-coded by child, and make sure each one understands what he is expected to do. Motivated students will feel free to move on without being reminded. This not only gives your children flexibility, but also gives them control over their day, teaches them management skills, and lets you oversee their work without nagging. Before long, your kids will realize that the sooner they finish their work, the sooner they can play or pursue other interests.

Multi-tasking

When planning your schedule, multi-task as much as possible. Combine a school activity with a home endeavor and save precious time. Read aloud while folding laundry or eating breakfast or lunch. You can take bites as you read, eat before or after your children, or eat really fast and then read! Reading during meals, or during other quiet pursuits, keeps distractions to a minimum and gives you more time during other parts of the day to work on other subjects.

Schedule multiple activities whenever possible. Have classical music tapes playing in the background during dinner. Listen to foreign language CDs in the car while going to dance class, and study the multiplication tables or spelling words while running errands. Keep the necessary tapes, CDs, and flashcards in the car so they will be handy when you need them.

Cover your kitchen table with a clear plastic table cloth and put interesting charts, maps, and posters under it. Keep flashcards and other fascinating reading materials in the bathroom. They can be completely unrelated to anything your children are currently studying, and the more unusual and interesting, the better. One of my daughters memorized the order of the planets simply because a science flashcard was lying on the stack of books in the bathroom.

Making the Schedule Work

Okay, so you have a schedule. Now implement your schedule and make it work. Here are ways to reduce interruptions and make the most of your time:

- Have every child go to the restroom before school starts.
- Keep the television off until all children have completed their work.
- Ask your family and friends to wait to call until school time is over.
- Take the phone off the hook, or turn off the ringer and let the answering machine pick up.
- If you must answer the phone, keep the call short.
- Put a "No Solicitors" sign on your door.

Because most of us are usually more alert in the morning, you may want to focus on the main subjects then. Save afternoons for group projects and independent work. On the other hand, some families prefer to get least favorite subjects out of the way first. When favorite subjects are saved for later in the day, their children have an incentive to complete the work they dislike. Try both suggestions, and see which one works for your family.

Encourage independent study. Of course, at first a young child will need you by her side reading directions and explaining new concepts. Sometime around second grade, however, she should be able to work independently after you have gone over the initial instructions. Sometimes all you will need to tell her are the page numbers. This will free you to work with other children and do household chores. Of course, remain nearby in case your child has questions, and check on her progress occasionally. If you are concerned that you may forget to check on older students studying in their bedrooms, set a timer to remind you.

Here are a few more suggestions to make your schedule work smoothly:

- **Get as much done for the morning as possible the night before.** Set the breakfast table, clear the kitchen counter and sinks, sort a load of laundry, and look over tomorrow's schedule.
- **Schedule a 15-minute break in the middle of lessons to let off some energy.** A few minutes to stretch or run around outside will help your children stay focused until lunch.
- **Plan a mid-morning snack.** Fruit, cheese and crackers, dry cereal, toast, and juice are quick, nutritious and easy to clean up.
- **Consider instituting a "quiet time" every day.** This is a mandatory time in the afternoon when all children retire to separate rooms to nap, play qui-

etly or read, depending on their ages. Not only will you benefit from the break, but also they will have a chance to play with their own toys without having to share or catch up on school work without interruption.

- **Correct school work each day.** In our family, Dad goes over the daily work with each child in the evening. Not only does this prevent the work to be corrected from piling up, but also the children reinforce what they have learned that morning, any mistakes are corrected early before bad habits have formed, and Dad stays involved in school.
- **Limit extracurricular activities so you are not constantly on the road.** Reduce your own commitments and allow each child only one extracurricular activity per week.
- **Evaluate your homeschool quarterly to ensure things are working out and to see if you are meeting your goals.** Then adjust your schedule as needed.

Homeschooling Through an Illness or Crisis

Sometimes life disrupts our schedules. We may have to deal with a high-risk pregnancy, an unexpected illness, a death in the family, a move to a new house, military deployment or the first few months with a newborn. Take time off when necessary, and don't feel guilty. Use that time to focus on enrichment activities, or label the time off as "school break" no matter when it falls on the calendar. If you have high school students, they should be responsible enough to continue their education without your constant presence anyway.

When you or the children are sick, focus on getting well. Don't worry about sticking to a schedule. Prioritize and do only the important things. Your kids may still be able to read books, keep a journal, pursue their hobbies, and do light chores. You could orally review their studies or do just the core subjects, such as reading and math. For example, when I broke my foot during my fourth pregnancy, we concentrated on each child's individual reading and math, and put everything else on the back burner for a while. Then we took two months off completely after the birth of each child. Your kids will quickly catch up when circumstances return to normal.

Use this interruption to your schedule as a "teachable moment." Give a close-up account of how you and the new baby are doing. Explain the developmental process of pregnancy, your upcoming hospital visit, and breastfeeding. If you have a broken bone, teach your kids about the bones of the body. If you are moving, learn about your new state or new hometown.

If you must be on the road a lot, take tote bags full of books, workbooks, notebooks, pencils, and paper, and "car school." Play games like "I Spy" and "20

Questions" and listen to audio tapes of books, foreign languages, multiplication, and geography. Keep CDs, flashcards, word games, logic puzzles, and mind games in the car for when you need them.

Here are a few more tips:

- **Keep your students on track with a schedule.** If you must go to bed for a few days or you need to pack, your kids can refer to the schedule on their own. Since you are home, you are still available for questions.
- **Rely on your husband.** He could work with the children when he is home.
- **Ask your older children to help.** They can read to their siblings, play games, and even "play school," even if they do not really stay on topic. Take this opportunity to teach preteens and teenagers to plan meals as well as cook them, make a grocery list, expand their housecleaning skills, take care of small children, and help you pack.
- **Get outside help.** Ask friends and relatives to help out, especially if they have offered. Perhaps a family with children of similar ages can include your children in their homeschool program, or a homeschool teenager can help with teaching and child care. All of these people can follow your schedule and go to you with questions.
- **Do what you can while resting on the couch or in bed.** Play board and card games; cuddle up and read to your children. Institute a family read aloud time if you don't already have one.
- **Purchase good educational videos and children's literature on tape.** You can also borrow them from the library and video store.
- **Let your children play learning games.** Find games that they can play together and on their own, such as board games, quiet educational toys, computer games, and free Web games. Young kids will like www.NickJr.com, www.PBSKids.com, www.Lego.com, www.BigIdeaFun.com, and www.PlayhouseDisney.com. Older kids will like www.Gamequarium.com and www.FunSchool.com.

Although they may not spend a lot of time on academics during this time, children learn other things, such as helping out when needed, taking care of sick persons or a new baby, doing laundry, and entertaining siblings. As a result, they become a little more considerate, independent, and responsible. These character virtues are just as important as academics.

Chapter 8

Homeschooling with Little Ones Underfoot

If you provide your toddler with appropriate toys and supplies, she will entertain herself.

Homeschooling with an infant, toddler or preschooler at home will be challenging, but not impossible. One of the benefits of homeschooling several children is that toddlers and preschoolers soak up information like sponges. Indeed, I never taught my three youngest children the alphabet, colors or numbers. Because they played in the room where we did school, they picked up on information intended for their older siblings. Another benefit is that older children can teach younger ones. Whether they play school, actually assist with school work, or just read bedtime stories, your older children are like teacher's aides living in the house with you.

Nevertheless, youngsters often crave attention just when your students need instruction time. To alleviate the problem somewhat, devote time to the little ones before you even start school each day. Read a story or play a game. If they get attention from mom for a while first, even for only 15 minutes, they will be more likely to play quietly while their brothers and sisters have a turn, especially if you are firm in your expectation of obedience. Toddlers and preschoolers are not too young to respect limits and obey their parents.

Nap Time and Quiet Time

Infants usually take morning and afternoon naps, giving you two periods in which to teach. Even toddlers usually take one nap a day. If you have two youngsters taking naps, try to synchronize or overlap their nap times as much as possible to ensure the greatest amount of time to spend with your students. For those no longer taking naps, consider instituting a mandatory "quiet time." During quiet time, they must stay in their rooms playing quietly while you teach or work on projects with your students. My three-year-old was content to have quiet time because I emphasized proudly that she was finally too old for naps; plus, the fact that she could play rather than sleep delighted her. Depending on your child's personality, you may have a battle of wills occasionally or even for the first few days, but your child will learn to obey your command to stay in her room during quiet time as long as you consistently insist on her obedience.

In addition to nap time and quiet time, take advantage of early bedtimes. When the baby goes to bed early in the evening, you can teach the older children before their bedtime.

Toddler-proof Your House

If you have had older children for a while, your house may not be as baby-proofed as it could be. Go through and toddler-proof again. Although dangerous chemicals, such as detergents, are probably out of reach, you need to ensure that small toys and personal belongings of older siblings are also out of reach. Appropriate containers stored on high shelves will solve this problem. Also, put child-proof locks on cabinets and drawers or replace the current ones that your bright toddler has already figured out. Purchase child-proof door handle locks for bedroom, bathroom and laundry room doors, and close those doors during school time. Use baby gates to block stairs and other areas of the house that are off limits to the toddler and preschooler during school. Put away all stools and ladders, except for one that only you can reach.

Including Little Ones During School Time

Include little ones during school when possible. Sit infants on your lap, carry them in a sling or backpack, and nurse if necessary. You may want to have diaper supplies, juice, a few toys, and a baby swing in the designated school room so you will not have to leave to get necessities for the baby.

Toddlers and preschoolers like to emulate older siblings and participate in group activities. Therefore, have the youngster sit in your lap or a sibling's lap when you read aloud. Put him in a high chair or booster seat at the table and give him crayons, coloring books, and paper to draw and color while his siblings do math. Preschool workbooks from discount stores will make your youngster feel as if he is doing school, too.

"School Time Only" Box

Keeping your toddler or preschooler busy during school time will ensure the greatest amount of instruction time with your students. You do not have to entertain him. Indeed, if he starts to expect to be entertained, he will be less likely to play on his own. On the other hand, if you provide him with appropriate toys and supplies, he will entertain himself.

Set aside a small table or floor area in the same room with you. Collect toys especially for your toddler or preschooler to play with, and rotate favorites to keep him interested. Since you will be focused on your students, do not give him items that are small enough to cause choking. Here are some suggestions for the "school time only" box:

- Modeling clay with plastic rolling pin and cookie cutters
- Paint books or watercolors and paper
- Coloring books and crayons
- Chalk on dark construction paper
- Chalk, slates or blackboard, and erasers
- Stencils, paper, colored pencils
- Safety scissors and paper
- Sticky notes and a pencil
- Retractable measuring tape
- Puzzles

- Picture books
- Stacking cups or containers of different sizes
- Pots, pans, bowls, and large plastic spoons
- Dry cereal and small bowls, cups or toy dump trucks
- Dry cereal and a shoelace to string a "necklace"
- Blocks of various sizes, colors, and shapes
- Magnet letters and a metal cookie sheet
- A large box big enough for him to get in and crayons to decorate it
- Empty laundry basket
- Discarded junk mail that has been opened and put back in envelopes
- An old purse or pillowcase to hold small toys (not plastic bags)
- Tent (a real camping tent or a tent made from blankets and a table and chairs)
- Creative play toys such as dolls, trucks, dress-up clothes, play foods, cars, and puppets

Collect these items into two different containers, and alternate the containers so the items will be "fresh" each time. Do not give your little one all the playthings at once; instead, select a toy for him, or let him pick one. Since you are familiar with your own child's abilities, do not put anything in the container that may frustrate rather than entertain him.

Educational Games and Programs

Your computer can entertain and teach, too. Purchase educational games designed just for toddlers and preschoolers, and allow access only during school time. Alternatively, take them online to play free learning games at www.NickJr.com, www.PBSKids.com, www.Lego.com, www.PlayhouseDisney.com, and www.BigIdeaFun.com. However, be sure to keep an eye on them so they will not venture off to other sites on the Internet.

Electronic toys and games are popular. Select games that teach as they entertain. Ask other homeschoolers what educational games their children like.

Use the television in an adjoining room as a last resort. Kids can watch educational programs on PBS or Nick Jr. or an educational video, such as the Veggie Tales™ videos by Big Idea Productions. You can find suitable movies to rent at any video store or library.

Getting Help from Others

You do not have to shoulder the responsibility alone. Enlist the help of others around you, such as your older children, spouse, friends, and relatives. Have older children take turns reading a story to or playing with the younger children for 20 to 45 minutes each day while you teach another child. The older children will benefit from the added responsibility, and the younger children will enjoy the special attention from their brothers and sisters.

Include your spouse. When he gets home from work or before he leaves for work, he can spend time with the baby while you school the older children. Alternatively, he can teach while you tend to the baby.

Some families hire a homeschooler as a babysitter for a few hours per week. Many high-school-aged homeschoolers seek part-time employment for a reasonable wage. You could even barter the babysitting time by tutoring math or teaching sewing.

Another option is to co-op babysitting duties with another family. Perhaps a neighbor can watch your toddler for an hour or two twice a week, and you can reciprocate on two other days. Your neighbor may be grateful for the uninterrupted school time if she homeschools, or she may just appreciate the chance to run errands or take an exercise class during that time.

Finally, ask extended family. Grandparents, aunts, and uncles can play with the baby or take him on outings. Such arrangements can forge strong and lasting relationships that probably would not have had an opportunity to grow if your children went to school.

Change Your Homeschooling Methods

If all else fails, you may need to change the way you homeschool for a year or two, especially if your children cannot study independently yet. Minimize academics and increase field trips. Join a field trip group. Take every opportunity to go out as much as possible. For instance, explore and play outdoors, go to museums, participate in sports, take classes at the YMCA, and go on family field trips. Your hometown probably has a variety of learning opportunities to explore; check the yellow pages and newspaper for ideas.

On the other hand, temporarily reducing outside interests may be best. After all, you will be unable to enjoy various activities and field trips if you have two little ones who need naps or if your toddler gets into everything. Instead, stay home, focus on school, and go on virtual field trips online. If you do school only when the baby sleeps, you will need to make the most of your limited time each day anyway. Rather than go to group activities, plan family activities and invite others to your house. Consider this time as an opportunity to foster strong sibling relationships.

This may be the best time to unschool your children for a while. Save structured academics for when your littlest ones are a bit older, especially if your children are in elementary grades and below. For now, just play, read books, sing songs, go on field trips, do simple crafts, cook, and bake, and let the little ones join in. Lay a good foundation of Bible stories, memory verses, and songs until they are ready to read, write, and do math. For your high school students, on the other hand, allow them all the freedom they want to pursue their interests while you are busy with the babies. Monitor their activities and be available for help as needed.

Chapter 9

If You Have Elementary and Middle Schoolers

Young students can learn to work independently.

You are probably homeschooling your young children already in ways you do not realize. Continue having them set the table, unload the dishwasher, and put away groceries. Talk with them as you do laundry, cook, clean house, and play together. Answer their many questions. Make the most of "teachable moments." Most of all, prepare your elementary and middle school students for independent learning now.

Preparing a Learning Environment

Independent learning begins with a learning environment where children of all ages enjoy learning all the time. A learning environment means lots of books, craft supplies, games, and creative toys all within easy reach. It also entails plenty of time for your children to indulge in various pursuits and interests on their own.

Actually, a traditional curriculum may bore young children. Instead, read books aloud, put puzzles together, memorize Bible verses, sing songs, and let them cook, bake, paint, and play. Be available to help when their enterprises go wrong and help them clean up when projects get finished. Their creative outlets may prove messy, such as spilled flour or paint, but the results will be impressive because they will finish their endeavors with a sense of accomplishment and confidence in themselves. And that is more important than a clean kitchen floor.

How To Avoid Busy Work

Even when you do use a traditional curriculum, vary your activities during the day and avoid the busy work that classroom teachers assign their students. Children enjoy hands-on activities in particular. Include music, creative interests, and physical pursuits along with sitting activities such as flashcards and workbooks. Also, your child does not have to do all the problems or answer all the questions. Your one-on-one instruction allows you to know if your child understands the work. Once he knows it, move on.

In addition, let him answer the questions orally or use a computer sometimes; lessons do not always have to be written down. The physical act of writing by hand can be time consuming and frustrating for some children. Allow your student to be the teacher occasionally; he reads the chapter and teaches it you. Also, don't feel that you have to cover every subject every day. Concentrate on reading, writing, and math, and add extra subjects or interesting projects a couple of days a week.

Be creative! Present information in a variety of ways. Using the alphabet as an example, concentrate on one letter at a time and:

- Show the letter on a flashcard.
- Have him write the letter with a pencil on paper.
- Get him to draw the letter on the driveway using sidewalk chalk.
- Point out the letter in stories and on signs.
- Have him color the letter in a coloring book.

- Let him hit the letter on the computer keyboard.
- Get him to make the letter out of beans, blocks, French fries or modeling clay.
- Let him write the letter in sand, pudding or shaving cream.
- Get him to make the shape of the letter with his hands or body.
- Play an "I Spy" game where the answer begins with that letter.
- Record your child saying the sound of the letter and play it back.

Present new concepts when your child is ready. If he seems uninterested, gets frustrated, or simply does not seem to "get it," set the material aside for a while and try again next month. By then, the concept just may click in his mind. He merely needs to go at his own speed. This also applies to his daily study pace. If one student works slowly, let him take as much time as he needs. Thanks to homeschooling, he will not be left behind. Similarly, if your four-year-old wants to read or your 10-year-old is ready for algebra, do not let their ages keep them from progressing. After all, one of the benefits of homeschooling is the flexibility that allows each child to progress when he is ready.

Help each child find his talents by helping him explore his interests, whether in academics or athletics. Be enthusiastic! Let him talk to others who are in that field or take classes to learn more. If he loses interest after a few months of tennis, that's okay. He was interested at one time, and he was able to pursue his interest. That is the only way he will find out where his talents lie.

Keeping Children Focused

Young children have short attention spans, so spend only about 10 to 15 minutes on any particular activity before moving on to the next one. Indeed, plan for no more than about 30 minutes of school in a day for preschoolers and kindergarteners. First and second graders should be able to handle about one hour of school work in a typical day, depending on the curriculum you choose. Elementary and middle school students will spend two to three hours. Even junior high and high school students will average three to four hours on focused school work in a day. This is plenty of time for all necessary subjects.

Although the time devoted to school work increases for the student as he gets older, the time needed for instruction by the parent decreases. In the early years, you will need to explain new concepts to your student, read directions, go over problems, and read chapters aloud. Eventually, he will read on his own, figure out the problems, and go to you only when needed. This usually begins around second or third grade, when a child can read directions on his own.

Your students will learn to work independently once they have learned to stay focused on a task. To train them to work on their own and to stay focused on their lessons, start with short assignments so they will not get frustrated, so they will gain confidence in themselves, and so they will learn to complete their lessons without you by their side all the time. Then gradually increase the size of the assignments. A list of lessons in priority order and a timer may help as well. Eliminate distractions by turning off the television, sending siblings to play in another room and instructing them to whisper.

With more than one child to homeschool, you need your children to work independently and to stay focused so you can devote one-on-one time with others as needed. However, even when students are working on their own, let them know you are available for help and check on them regularly. Set a timer to remind you if necessary.

Talking and Reading to Children

Talking with children is an essential element to homeschooling successfully. Engage them in conversation. Answer their many questions. You can work on your children's grammar simply by repeating what they say in correct form. You can also increase their vocabulary by varying yours and explaining words they do not know.

Reading to them is just as important as talking with them. Schedule regular time to read aloud from good books just for fun. Even preteens and teenagers still like to be read to, especially from good books. Build a home library of classics and quality books. Although you may be reading aloud from these books now, your children will likely choose to read them later on their own.

The Importance of Playtime

Play is children's work and is just as important to their development as academics, so give your children plenty of time to play with their siblings, friends, and by themselves. Provide board games, art and craft supplies, and creative playthings.

Play with your children yourself and enjoy them at these young ages. You do not have to be their entertainment; on the contrary, your children should learn to entertain themselves. However, you can join in their play occasionally and include them in your activities when possible. Read books together, play board games, do crafts, bake together, and include them when you pursue your hobbies, if possible. These are wonderful opportunities to get to know your children and have them get to know you.

To find age peers for your children, join a local homeschool support group or neighborhood playgroup. A support group offers youngsters a variety of social opportunities, such as field trips, park days, and clubs, where they can play and make new friends among other homeschoolers. A playgroup offers similar opportunities for toddlers and preschoolers. For information about homeschool groups and playgroups, refer to Chapter 14.

Chapter 10

Handling Junior High and High Schoolers

*High school students can devise their own
daily schedules.*

You can homeschool your junior high and high school students successfully, even if you have more than one at the same time. You may prefer a packaged curriculum or a more relaxed approach using the library and Internet. Do what is best for each individual student, keeping in mind state requirements for graduation and each child's plans for higher education and career.

If your high school students are close in age, you can plan their subjects simultaneously. After all, one of the benefits of homeschooling is the flexibility that allows you to teach each child different subjects on separate grade levels and permits each child to progress at his own pace. As a result, if two students are only one grade apart, for example, they can study the same materials and graduate together. On the other hand, if they are not close enough in age to teach them the same material at the same time, at least they may be far enough apart not to be in high school at the same time. This has been the case with Pam, allowing her to focus on a comprehensive college-prep curriculum for one student at a time.

Generally, a high school student should be self-sufficient, and a junior high student should be well on the way to self-sufficiency. Assignments should be done in a reasonable amount of time. For both junior high and high school students, be available to provide guidance, help them find books and mentors, and discuss news and literature together, but allow them to proceed on their own. After all, you are preparing these young adults for independence and for a lifetime of learning, whether in college or employment.

High School Requirements

Some states mandate certain subjects, credit hours, and exit exams for home-school graduates. Find out what your state requires while each student is in junior high so that you will be able to plan his high school years appropriately. Most parents of high school students work backwards from their students' goals, whether that happens to be college, apprenticeship, or employment, and design a course of study to achieve their ambitions.

If your high school student plans for college, find out the admission requirements for the schools he is considering. Contact their admissions departments or check their Web sites. According to the College Board, most institutions require four years of English, including literature and composition; three years of social studies; three years of math, including Algebra I and higher; two years of science and one lab, not including general science; and three years of additional credits, such as two years of a foreign language and other electives. Once you know what is required, use the high school years to cover the necessary subjects and take the standardized tests.

Most institutions require certain scores on the SAT (formerly Scholastic Aptitude Test) or ACT (formerly American College Testing) or other college entrance exams. Prepare your student for taking these standardized tests by using guides you can find in bookstores and online. Most recommend that students should study algebra and geometry by the end of their junior year in preparation for taking college entrance tests. If your student will be taking the exams early, make sure he has taken these two math courses early as well.

Various books and guides help determine courses of study for high school students. The Internet, too, is a valuable resource. For example, www.WorldBook.com provides a typical course of study categorized by grade level, subjects, and topics. Information on materials and activities help parents cover the subjects and check mastery of the skills.

Keep in mind that every subject does not have to be mastered, but exposure to the subject will make college easier. Good note-taking skills will also make college easier. Have your high school student take notes from history and science books. To get experience with taking notes from a lecture, enroll your student in a lecture class through a homeschool co-op or junior college, or perhaps have him take notes during your pastor's sermons.

Handling Difficult Subjects

Don't worry about teaching difficult subjects to your high school student. The Internet provides ample information, and numerous books are available at the library on a variety of reading levels. You can always learn along with your student; for example, order a foreign language program and learn together. Teacher's manuals explain what you need to know and may even present different ways to explain difficult concepts to your child. As a result, if you order a packaged curriculum, be sure to purchase the accompanying teacher's manuals.

Video courses are another option. For subjects like math and science, an actual teacher explains the material step-by-step, and your students can review sections over and over as needed. Pam, mother of three, has used video courses to teach high school biology and chemistry successfully.

Think about the skills and talents your friends and family may be willing to share. Your uncle may be a math whiz, so he can teach calculus. Your sister may have majored in English in college, so she can grade essays. Also, you could engage a retired school teacher, homeschooling parent or college student to tutor challenging subjects. Check your local homeschool group for a list of possible tutors.

Here are additional options that other families have found successful:

- **Local experts often teach art and musical instruments.** Check the yellow pages and your local newspaper, and ask around.
- **Homeschool driving programs provide the necessary paperwork, videos, and online instruction.** Check out www.DriverEdTraining.com, www.DriverzEd.com, and www.NationalDriverTraining.com. You could also enroll your teen in a local driving school; check the yellow pages for listings. Find out your state laws and automobile insurance requirements before you order or enroll in a program to avoid wasting time and money.

- **Homeschool support groups and umbrella schools often organize co-op classes on difficult subjects.** Refer to Chapter 14 for more information on co-ops.
- **Homeschool juniors and seniors can take classes at junior colleges.** In many cases, a junior and senior can earn college and high school credit simultaneously.
- **Tutorials are available on the Internet.** Try www.AlexandriaTutorials.com, www.GBT.org, www.NetTutor.com, www.OxfordTutorials.com, and www.Schola-Tutorials.com. You can also search the Internet for others.
- **Interactive online high school classes are also available.** Two such online high schools are www.Northstar-Academy.org and www.PottersSchool.com, but you can search on "interactive online high school classes" for a list of others.
- **Take a correspondence course.** The student mails completed lessons, which a teacher will grade. Search online for "homeschool correspondence course" or "distance learning."

Another viable option is to find a mentor to stimulate and challenge your young adult once his specific field of study becomes clear. A mentor is not a tutor, but a professional who acts as your teenager's adviser and role model. You can find suitable candidates by consulting professional societies and community organizations in the particular field of study in which your student is interested.

College Preparation

A variety of guides furnish parents with information on preparing students for college admission and keeping track of necessary paperwork. Check the library, bookstores, and Internet. For example, www.CollegeBoard.com provides academic planning for college-bound students; www.HomeschoolFriendlyColleges.com furnishes a list of colleges and universities that admit homeschoolers, and www.TodaysFreebies.com offers a booklet on financial aid.

As already mentioned, check with the institution that your child is interested in and find out what is required for admission of homeschoolers besides certain subjects and minimum test scores on the SAT or ACT. Requirements vary, but schools may require a diploma, General Equivalency Diploma (GED), and transcript.

According to the Home School Legal Defense Association (HSLDA), home-schoolers can "self-certify" the completion of their high school program just as public and private schooled graduates self-certify that they have received a diploma. Homeschoolers do not have to take the GED, and admissions officers should not require any form of third party corroboration. Also, homeschoolers are eligible for federal financial aid. For more information, contact HSLDA or go to www.HSLDA.org. If your homeschool graduate wants a diploma to hang on his wall, you can purchase or print your own from several sites on the Internet, such as www.HomeschoolDiploma.org. Or simply search on "homeschool diploma."

Since colleges and universities use a high school transcript more than a diploma to evaluate a student's college potential, you will need to prepare a transcript for your college-bound student. A transcript is simply a list of subjects, the grades received, and the units each course is worth. Translate whatever your student has learned into terms the educational community can understand, such as math and language arts. Be specific, such as "chemistry" rather than "science." Give grades based on what the student accomplished. Just as with a diploma, transcripts are easy to find on the Internet; search on "homeschool transcript."

However, since homeschoolers may not be able to demonstrate their college potential through transcripts alone, many institutions also rely on portfolios, interviews, and letters of recommendation from tutors, mentors, junior college professors, and community leaders who have worked with the students. Furthermore, apprenticeships, independent projects, competitions, publications, volunteer work, and mission activities will make a difference as well.

In addition, most universities will accept homeschoolers with 12 to 36 credits of community college work already completed. In fact, most community colleges offer a "dual enrollment" program in which high school students can take classes to earn both college and high school credits at the same time. The admission requirement is usually a certain minimum score on the SAT, ACT, or the school's College Placement Test. Contact your local junior college for requirements.

Taking a few basic college courses will prepare your teenager for full-time college and may even help boost his SAT or ACT scores. Sign up for classes that will meet most colleges' general education requirements to ensure that the credits will transfer to the four-year institution of your child's choice. Before registering for a class, try to find out about the professor, so you can avoid those who show up late for classes, cancel labs, and use only multiple choice tests.

Another option for homeschoolers to get a head start on college is to take CLEP (College Level Examination Program) and AP (Advanced Placement) exams. Both are viable ways to earn college credits through testing in certain subjects. Go to www.DavidAndLaurie.com for CLEP study guides. Most colleges and universities grant CLEP and AP credits. Go to www.CollegeBoard.com for details.

Homeschoolers are also eligible for scholarships. For information about available scholarships, check with local colleges and the Adult Education Department of large city libraries.

Alternatives to College

If your child does not plan to attend college, then his high school subjects are up to you and your child. He may need consumer math rather than calculus, for example. However, you still should tailor his courses to fit his goals after graduation. You will find plenty of resources from the library and Internet on alternatives to college and how to prepare academically.

Your high school student has several viable choices besides college. Indeed, college is not always the best option for everyone, especially if your child does not have a specific career goal in mind. Some homeschoolers join the military or enter the mission field. Some prefer a technical or trade school for training in a specialized career; check the yellow pages for schools near you. Others opt to travel through student and work exchange programs; search on the Internet for reputable organizations and programs.

Some homeschoolers choose apprenticeships or internships. As a matter of fact, depending on the field, an apprenticeship may be better than college. Through an apprenticeship, a student learns under a master in the trade, skill, or career in which he is interested and at which he is talented. When setting up an apprenticeship position, look for a local business or an individual who is well known for integrity in business practices and for quality of work.

Also, keep in mind that college always remains an option, whether one year or five years later. Most colleges and universities highly value older students because they are usually enthusiastic, self-directed, and focused on learning.

Part Time Jobs and Volunteer Work

Before and during college, your high school student could invest his time wisely in a part time job, missions work, and community service. Instead of working at the mall, encourage your teen to find ways of making money that fit his interests, skills, and schedule. Depending on where you live and on his abilities, he may find a job helping at the library, guiding tours at a museum, teaching swimming, or working for a small business or your church. Check the yellow pages for small businesses related to your teenager's interests.

If he has found the ideal place to work, but the potential employer cannot afford to hire anyone, perhaps your teen can intern for free. Many teenagers start off volunteering and then move on to paid part-time or full-time positions.

A resourceful teenager may even start his own business. The enterprise does not have to be anything big and permanent yet; most self-employed teens simply take advantage of available opportunities. He or she could provide a service, such as tutoring, babysitting, being a mother's helper, pet sitting, mowing lawns, cleaning pools, cleaning houses, or shoveling snow. Your teenager may even be able to sell a product he makes or sell someone else's handiwork.

Be aware of the pros and cons of working part time, whether self-employed or for a business. Although your student will have less free time, he will have a sense of accomplishment and his own money. Furthermore, he will learn to deal with the issues of working, such as being on time, handling office politics, and coping with patrons.

Find out the state laws related to working minors, and then research the job before agreeing to let your child take a position. Investigate the job hours, pay, and benefits as well as the manager and co-workers. After all, your child will be spending several hours a week with these people, so you need to be sure that the environment is safe.

As a homeschooler available during the day, your student has a unique opportunity to spend considerable time in volunteer positions as well as in ministry. Check with local hospitals, retirement and nursing homes, and charitable and political organizations. Missions work through your local house of worship may also be an option. In any case, volunteer and ministry work can provide an impressive resume as well as great references and work experience.

Chapter 11

Single Parents and Working Parents

*Single and working parents trade books, childcare, and
even meals to help meet the challenges of homeschooling.*

For single parents and working parents, homeschooling more than one child
will be challenging, but not impossible. You may find that you cannot do everything that other homeschooling families with one child or one parent at home
do. You will probably have fewer playdates and extracurricular activities.
Nevertheless, working and single parents can and do homeschool successfully.
You simply have to find the method that works best for your family.

Sit down with your spouse and determine together what you feel are the most
important subjects for your children to learn, then prioritize your homeschooling

to accommodate your decisions. For instance, if math and language arts are important, schedule them every day. Put other subjects on the back burner temporarily, or cover them only once or twice a week. Once you have prioritized, you can tackle other concerns.

Your Work Schedule

If feasible, take your children to work with you. Reading and workbooks can be done quietly at many locations, and your children may be able to help at the office by stuffing envelopes or shredding paper. Then you could spend a couple of hours each night on instruction and the weekends on projects and field trips.

If your children cannot go to work with you, check state laws for the age at which a child may stay home without adult supervision. Those who are old enough can study at home during the day using books, workbooks, educational computer programs, and online classes. One-on-one instruction with you can be scheduled in the evenings and on weekends. If you follow this plan, devise a contract that specifically details what you expect from your preteen and teenager. That way, they know exactly what they must do in each subject and how their work will be graded. Your limited time together can then be spent mostly in discussion of their work.

Children in elementary and primary grades may have to wait until you get home from work to do school. Since they should be able to complete school work in an hour or so a day, you could set aside an hour when you are home for such subjects as math, reading, handwriting, and history. As long as they have time to play, explore nature, go to the library, do chores, and do crafts with their sitters, they will still be learning.

Here are a few more suggestions to carve out school time around work:

- **Stagger your work hours with your spouse.** He works while you are home, and you work while he is home. Either designate one of you as the sole teacher or divide the teaching load.
- **School around your work.** If you have a seasonal job or you work only a few months of the year, schedule school for months that business is slower or for months that you do not work.
- **Consider schooling year-round.** If your state requires a certain number of school days per year, you will have ample time to meet state requirements.

Family and Friends

It may be easy to isolate yourself when work and homeschool take up so much time, but try to be involved with people around you. Stay in touch with neighbors, friends, and relatives. Let them help and support you rather than try to carry the burden alone. Trade carpool favors, childcare, books, curricula, and even meals with other families to help relieve the burden on you. Seek other working and single parent homeschoolers through a local homeschool group or Internet email group.

You could even enlist the help of close friends and family to homeschool your children. A friend or relative could teach one or two subjects to the children. Perhaps a family with children of similar ages can temporarily include your children in their homeschool program, or a homeschool teenager can help with teaching and child care. Your older children could study independently and help with the younger children, and babysitters could provide creative activities for the kids in addition to free play time.

Older Children

Some working parents allow their teenagers to take part-time jobs or apprenticeships in their chosen field during work hours. The teens gain experience and earn their own money. Alternatively, your teenagers could do school work and keep up the house as well as babysit and teach the younger children while you are at work. Also, once your teens can drive, let them know that they will be expected to chauffeur siblings, get groceries, and run errands occasionally.

If your children will be home alone while you are at work, make a rule that no-one is allowed in the house if a parent is not at home. Then stay connected by cell phone, telephone, and email. Prepare a phone list of neighbors or relatives who can serve as backups if you cannot be reached in an emergency. If you will be unavailable for any reason during the day, call your children and remind them to call the backup person if an emergency arises.

Work-at-Home Possibilities

Investigate the feasibility of telecommuting or cutting back to part-time. Alternatively, start a home-based business, such as consulting, designing Web sites, freelance writing, tutoring, giving music lessons, sewing clothes, selling scrapbook supplies or home decor, baking cakes, or running a home daycare. Find a way to make money from a skill or talent. Your children will benefit from helping you run a home-based business.

If you work at home, gather materials that your students can use during your work hours. Here are a few suggestions:

- **Obtain books on tape from the library or bookstore.** Invest in earphones for each child.

- **Select quality videos to replace television programs.** Both video stores and libraries may have documentaries and cartoons on famous people and historic events.

- **Buy educational computer games or play Web games.** Young children will enjoy www.Lego.com, www.NickJr.com, www.PBSKids.com, www.PlayhouseDisney.com, and www.BigIdeaFun.com. Older kids will like www.Gamequarium.com and www.FunSchool.com.

- **Try non-messy crafts.** Children can color, make potholders, and string beads to make necklaces. Go to www.TheIdeaBox.com for more suggestions.

As long as legal requirements are met, a single parent or two working parents can homeschool their multiple children successfully. Some days will be busier than you would like, but you should be able to manage with a little forethought and help from family and friends.

Chapter 12

The Juggling Act: Housework and Homeschool

Giving children household responsibilities is a necessity in running a large household.

Many people question, "How do you find time to homeschool and keep your house functioning?" A little time management and organization go a long way, even with a house full of children all day.

Prioritizing for Maximum Efficiency

With several children who need your time and attention, you cannot do everything, so accept your limitations and focus on important matters. Pam and her husband, who have three children, agree that homeschooling comes first, recreation a much-needed second, and housework a distant third. Like Pam, once you have set priorities, everything else falls into place.

Prioritize your housecleaning, too. If clean floors mean a clean house to you, then make vacuuming and mopping your cleaning priorities. On the other hand, if clutter drives you nuts, schedule time to pick up in the morning, after dinner, and before bedtime. Perhaps having tidy public rooms is important because family and friends tend to pop in unexpectedly. In that case, devote day-to-day housecleaning to public living areas, such as the living room, kitchen, and guest bathroom. Alternatively, ask your husband what he appreciates most, and focus on that area on those days when you don't have time for everything.

Once you have prioritized, you may need to lower your standards and expectations. You cannot expect a house full of children all day to be spotless! Settle for picked up, rather than spic-and-span clean. You may even need to adjust your definition of "clean." For instance, when I broke my foot while pregnant with our fourth child, I quickly realized that a clean kitchen floor means two different things depending on whether your youngest child is eight months old or eight years old. I also learned that not all clothes need to be ironed, dishes can air dry until the next day, and there is more than one way to fold and put away towels. Another valuable lesson: Children as young as two can do their share of housecleaning.

Chores

Giving children household responsibilities is a necessity in running a large household. Doing their share is as important as academics because children learn such character virtues as responsibility, diligence, thoroughness and teamwork. If you begin at an early age, helping around the house will be a normal part of each day to your children, especially if you make chores as fun as possible, keep them age-appropriate, and do them together as a team.

Victoria trains her children to learn each job as they get older and has them take turns doing the work. Her primary goal is to teach her seven children to be helpful, cheerful, loving and responsible as they learn to take care of their own clothes, possessions, and space. Like Victoria, teach your young children to set the table, load and empty the dishwasher, empty the dryer, dust, sweep, and put away toys. Older kids can do more complex chores such as sorting, starting, folding, and putting away laundry as well as ironing, cooking simple meals, vacuuming, and mopping.

Although children sometimes need to do chores they do not like in order to learn discipline, you may want to assign some tasks to those who do them best and with less whining and complaining; this will certainly alleviate some stress in your household. In any case, avoid gender-specific chores so that both boys and girls do laundry and cook as well as cut grass and take out the trash. After all, you are teaching each child to become a self-sufficient adult who is prepared for life, not a person who needs a partner to function properly.

Clearly define chore routines by writing them out in detail or using pictures for pre-readers. Keep a chore chart in a central location so that each child knows his responsibilities and so you can tell when a task has been neglected. Paper and dry-erase charts are available at office supply stores, discount stores, and online. Alternatively, design your own chart.

Instead of assigned chores, you could allot specific rooms or areas of your home. For example, put one child in charge of the living room, another in the den, one in the dining room, and another in the kitchen. They are responsible for all the picking up, dusting, sweeping, mopping, and vacuuming in their own designated rooms, which rotate on a daily, weekly or monthly basis. This method works best for our family. Also, if you have several children, consider dividing the chores in such a way that a different child gets a day off each Sunday.

Some families offer small prizes as incentives for chores consistently and cheerfully done well and in a timely manner. They hide coins or pieces of candy for a child to find while dusting. Instant rewards! One mom in our homeschool group lists the chores each night. Then the first child up and dressed the next morning gets his choice. Needless to say, he will pick the easiest, but that is his reward for getting up first. Other families devise a point system for chores, and at the end of each week the total points are cashed in for coins or extra television or computer time.

No matter how you assign household tasks, have everyone do quick chores before starting school and before leaving the house. Spend a few minutes to pick up the house and start a load of laundry. This method works best for Anita and her family. With all four of her children pitching in, the house is straight in no time and they are out the door or ready to start school.

At the end of the school day, have everyone put all school materials away before anyone can go anywhere, invite anyone over, eat a snack, watch television or play. One mom in our homeschool group goes a step further. Every evening she bags any items left lying around, and at the end of the week her children have to pay a quarter for the return of each item. If they do not have a quarter, they must earn one. Anita periodically uses this system when her four children lapse into leaving clothes lying on the bathroom or bedroom floors.

On regular clean-up days or quick pick-ups, work along with your children. Sing a clean-up song, play lively music or race around trying to beat a timer! No-one can complain because they see you cleaning, too. Plus, you set a good example for your children. As Pam's family does, declare a school holiday if necessary to get the house in order before guests arrive. After cleaning together, figure out the time it took all of you, and then figure out the time if there had been only one person. This underscores the importance of teamwork and sneaks in a little math!

Team up the kids by assigning each young child to an older brother or sister. This successful method is described in the classic book by Frank B. Gilbreth and Ernestine Gilbreth Carey, *Cheaper by the Dozen*, based on their growing up in a family of 12 children. The older child helps his younger sibling prepare his breakfast, get dressed, clean his room, get ready for bed, etc. As a result, each older child learns responsibility, each younger child develops new skills, and you are free to do something else. This method has always worked well in our family.

Here are a few more suggestions for housekeeping with multiple children:

- **Train your children to pick up their own messes.** Be consistent and set a good example.
- **Solve the problem of a bad attitude by assigning extra work.** Mandate cheerful obedience. Whoever whines or complains or is not cooperating gets the extra work that no one likes to do, such as cleaning out the refrigerator or reorganizing the kitchen cabinets.
- **Make housework easier by getting rid of possessions you don't need.** You and your children should periodically clean out your rooms, especially before birthdays and Christmas. One mom in our homeschool group keeps toy clutter under control by having her children choose a toy to throw away or give away for every new toy throughout the year.
- **Organize your housework.** Two popular systems are www.FlyLady.com and *Managers Of Their Homes* by Steve and Teri Maxwell at www.Titus2.com.
- **Hire a maid or cleaning service once a week or twice a month.** A homeschooler may do the job for less than a professional and would appreciate the money. You may find that the cost is worth the extra time to spend with your children.

Laundry

Laundry takes a lot of time in a large family, so delegate as much as possible to the children. A mom in our homeschool group assigns each child a different day to help with the family wash. In both Anita's and Pam's families, each child who turns 10 years old is placed in charge of his own laundry. As the children get older and more particular about their clothes, their mothers do not have to remember which items are washed only in cold water and never placed in the dryer.

In our family, the 12-year-old becomes in charge of "general" laundry, such as towels, sheets, and undergarments—all articles that cannot be ruined—while younger siblings are responsible for folding and putting them away. Although they do not wash and dry their own clothes, our children do sort their own clothes, fold, and put them away. As our children are conveniently spaced three years apart, once one child "graduates" to washing her own clothes at 15 years old, the next child just happens to be 12 years old and moves up to general laundry.

In addition to delegating laundry to your children, cut down on laundry as much as possible. Train children to hang up clothes after wearing them unless they are truly dirty so they can be worn more than once. A mom in our home-school group assigns each of her children a certain color for towels, and each towel must be hung up and used twice before washing. This reduces the washing load and allows her to identify anyone who leaves a towel on the floor.

Here are a few more laundry tips for a large family:

- **Place hampers in each bedroom and bathroom.** Require your children to use them.
- **Fold and put away each load immediately.** Alternatively, place a basket for each child near the dryer and put dried clothes straight into the baskets for the children to fold and put away.
- **Make folding laundry a group endeavor and include school activities.** While the kids are folding, read aloud to them or listen to foreign language tapes or classical music CDs.
- **Go through closets and drawers periodically and give away items that are no longer worn.** This will make room to put away those clothes that are worn.
- **Designate a different day for each type of laundry.** Leave the weekends free as motivation and reward for completing laundry during the week.

Meals

Meals create a lot of work in a large family, so plan them in advance. Think about dinner in the morning and defrost something during the day. Better yet, plan your menu a week ahead, so you do not have to worry from day to day and you can purchase ingredients in bulk or on sale. If you invest in a freezer, you can shop for groceries once a month and freeze most of them. Then the only provisions to be purchased weekly are perishables such as milk and fruit.

Simplify your meals. Serve toast, fruit, cereal or oatmeal for breakfast, and sandwiches, wraps, soup or salads for lunch. Stock a supply of quick microwavable meals. Prepare simple meals for supper four nights a week, and limit elaborate dishes to three nights a week. Leftovers make great lunches when warmed up the next day, or create a new dish with your leftovers. For example, turn last night's baked chicken into today's chicken salad.

Have each child prepare his own breakfast and lunch, so you do not have to serve as short order cook. Put each older child in charge of a little one; he prepares the breakfast, lunch, and drink for his charge and tidies up afterwards. If you have only one little child in the bunch, assign his meal preparation to one older sibling, his drink to another, and cleanup to another.

Here are creative ways to save time and labor in meal preparations:

- **Use a crock pot. Slow cookers are simple to use and easy to clean.** For recipes and cooking tips, go to www.CrockeryKitchen.com and www.TastyCrockPotRecipes.com.

- **Cook a month's worth of meals in one day and freeze them for later.** Known as "bulk cooking" or "freezer cooking," this method not only saves time in preparation and cleanup each day, but also saves money because you buy ingredients in bulk. Go to www.Hometown.AOL.com/OAMCloop and www.30DayGourmet.com to learn more and get recipes. Several books are available for delicious recipes that freeze and reheat well.

- **Double or triple the recipes and freeze portions for next week.** If your family dislikes "leftovers," simply transfer portions of the meal to containers and freeze them before your family sits down to eat. Because they will not have seen you put anything in the freezer, they will not consider next week's meals to be leftovers.

- **Have everyone pitch in to help with meal preparation.** Someone peels the potatoes and someone sets the table, while another prepares the drinks. After dinner, one child clears while another loads the dishwasher and another wipes the counters.

- **Assign one night a week when older children must cook.** Each one takes a different night or they team up to prepare supper together. The younger children clean up afterwards.

To reduce dishwashing loads, mark cups and dishes with the owner's initials in permanent ink. Better yet, assign colors to each child and purchase dishwasher-safe and microwaveable plastic cups and plates in the appropriate colors. Children must wash and reuse their cups and dishes all day until the after-supper dishwashing load. Color-coding makes children responsible for their own dishes, reduces the number of dirty dishes, and eliminates misunderstandings when dishes are left out. This has been very successful in our home. Another helpful tip: Use paper plates sometimes!

Other Tips

A homeschooling parent has many other responsibilities besides teaching, such as grocery shopping, going to medical appointments, returning library books, and running errands. To save time, combine chores whenever you go out so you will not waste time and gasoline running errands several times a week. Schedule appointments around school time, and if you run out of something, make do if possible rather than dash out to the grocery store just to pick up one or two items.

If you take your children along on errands or to appointments, bring school work for them to do while waiting or in transit. That's what car schooling is all about! Prepare a book bag with workbooks, worksheets, spelling lists, coloring books, flashcards, and books.

Carpool with friends to field trips, dance classes, and soccer practices, so you will not have to load everyone in the minivan for every practice. You will have extra time to catch up on housework or to spend with the remaining children doing school work. It will also save gasoline.

Finally, eliminate or reduce television time. Schedule the programs to watch. Keep the television off until that particular program comes on, and then turn it off again as soon as the program ends to keep from being drawn into the next show. Consider instituting a "No T.V. Day" once a week if you cannot eliminate television altogether. You will be surprised how productive and creative your family is when watching television is not an option.

Chapter 13

Staying Motivated and Preventing Burnout

Parents need motivation and encouragement just as much as their children do.

Children are born to learn, but sometimes they need motivation. Actually, you as an adult are no different. Especially with several children at home, you will sometimes need inspiration, motivation, and encouragement even more than your children will. Both children and adults will benefit from these suggestions.

Setting Goals

Keep in mind your reasons for homeschooling as you set goals for the year. You may decide on separate goals for each child. After all, one child may want to learn to read, another may need to catch up on math, and still another must finish a required college-prep course. As a family, you may want to read the Bible in one year or study world history. You may set a long-range goal of preparing your children to qualify for college scholarships by the end of high school, as Pam has done with her children. In any case, once you have identified your reasons for homeschooling and set your goals for the year, you can plan what to do to reach those goals, such as purchase a certain curriculum or spend more time on a particular subject.

Then divide your plan into semesters, quarters or months. With smaller portions to work with, you will not feel so overwhelmed. Refer to your goals frequently to remind you why you are homeschooling and to make sure you stay on track. As you accomplish each monthly or quarterly set of goals in your plan, you and your children will feel motivated to continue.

The same goes for weekly and daily goals. Perhaps organize your week on Sunday evening. Determine which days will be reserved for errands and what projects and extracurricular activities are scheduled this week. Then each night, spend about 30 minutes gathering materials and preparing for the next day. Consult your master list and write a checklist for the day on a chart or dry erase board. During the day, erase or mark off items as they are completed. This will give you a sense of accomplishment each day, keep you focused on your goals, and motivate you to continue.

The same may be said about to-do lists for students. One of my daughters thought that I would just give her another assignment when she completed a lesson, so she was not motivated to finish quickly. With a list of assignments to complete as her goal, she realized that she would be done at a certain point, which motivated her to work diligently.

Get Your Children Excited About Learning

Once you have set your goals for the year, motivate your students for the new school year by throwing a "back-to-homeschool" party for them and their friends with balloons, games, and a cake. Alternatively, host an open house for your relatives and friends—both homeschooling and non-homeschooling—to see your new books, calendar of field trips, supplies for projects and science experiments, and the special school area.

Here are a few more ideas for making the first day special:

- **Go out to breakfast on the first day.** One family in our homeschool group turns the outing into an experiment by comparing syrups at a favorite pancake restaurant.
- **Eat out for supper the first night.** Even though we homeschool year-round, our family goes out to our favorite restaurant to celebrate the start of each new school year.
- **Shop for new book bags and supplies.** Kids will look forward to using their new materials.
- **Spend the first day going through the new books, but not doing any lessons.** This will get all of you excited about the things you will read and do this year.
- **Decorate special T-shirts to commemorate the first day of school.** Do this either in addition to school work or in place of school work the first day.
- **Dress up your children and take individual pictures.** You and your children will enjoy looking back to see how they have grown through the years.

In addition to celebrating the new school year, use your children's natural curiosity to get and keep them enthusiastic. Showing interest in any topic your children ask about gets them excited about learning. Let your children make some of the decisions on what to study. Brainstorm together for ideas for projects and field trips, and be open to their suggestions.

You will not be able to satisfy each desire; most likely, one child will want to study insects, while another will want to learn about magnets, and still another will be interested in dinosaurs. Simply start with the youngest child's suggestion and progress to each topic in turn. Tell each child that in order for him to be assured that his topic will be done, he must be patient and participate cheerfully in the study of his siblings' choices. Of course, if he does not cooperate, you must follow through and skip his turn. Once he realizes that you mean what you say, he will change his attitude.

How to Make Learning Fun

In addition to encouraging student input, make school interesting by varying your activities during the day and including hands-on activities and field trips. Do more than just read books and write reports. Projects, tours, virtual field trips, dramas, puppet shows, songs, experiments, and board games provide a break from lessons and make learning fun. Include movies by going to www.TeachWithMovies.org for films that entertain and teach history, science, and literature.

Nurture a love of learning and create a learning environment. Provide plenty of writing materials, project supplies, and good books on various reading levels that your children will want to read. Instead of textbooks, choose "living books," such as historical novels, biographies, and classics. Leave these items out where your kids can access them even during non-school hours.

Make the most of field trips! Introduce the topics beforehand to arouse your students' natural curiosity and prepare them for what they will see. Depending on the destination and your children's ages, read stories about fire fighters for a trip to a fire station, research tides from the Internet before going to the beach, or write a letter to grandma to mail while touring the post office. Additionally, check the location's Web site for interesting facts and free lesson plans.

Extend and deepen the field trip experience after you return home. Have your students write about what they discovered; pre-writers can narrate or draw a picture. Read books related to the trip, do a craft or experiment, and research more information on the Internet. Share highlights with other family members at dinner that evening and when the photos are developed. Indeed, photos and other mementos, such as souvenirs, maps, and brochures, make meaningful keepsakes for children. Assemble them into a collage or scrapbook to preserve the fun memories indefinitely. If your state requires a portfolio, add them to it.

Here are a few more suggestions to make learning fun for all ages:

- **Break up the day with exercise.** Turn on lively music and dance, or walk around the block. Boys especially need physical outlets. Have them take the dog for a run, ride a bike around the block a few times, swim a few laps, play basketball or climb a tree.

- **Do the unexpected occasionally.** Do school outside on the first warm day of spring or cuddle up on your master bed to read history aloud. Similarly, read aloud on a pile of pillows or inside a fort made of blankets and chairs.

- **Keep samples of each child's work and periodically let him review his progress.** Seeing his improvements in handwriting, creative writing or timed math assignments will build his self-esteem and inspire him to continue working hard. This often works better than assigning grades.

- **Cut out "busy work."** If a child knows how to do the math problems, don't make him do the whole page. Allow him to answer history questions orally or on the computer sometimes. Let him teach you occasionally; quizzing you reinforces what he has learned. Plus, it's fun!

- **Let each child determine his daily schedule.** Give students their own to-do lists of assignments, but let each student decide which one to do first. Middle school through high school students, in particular, should be given the responsibility and freedom to design their own daily schedules with some assistance from you when needed.
- **Determine each child's learning style.** Each one may have a different style, but using his learning style will make education more interesting for him and less frustrating for you.

While education can be fun, it also entails hard work. After all, learning grammar rules and memorizing multiplication tables are not fun. Although you may implement games and songs, your students still must learn the necessary concepts. Instead of feeling like a failure in making school fun, look at these situations as character training. After all, education also involves acquiring such character virtues as diligence, patience, and self-discipline.

Handling Sibling Rivalry

Your children will have many opportunities to practice various character virtues as they live with their brothers and sisters on a day-to-day basis. They will also learn how to get along, negotiate, compromise, and resolve conflicts. With children at home all day, you will definitely face quarreling and fighting. Just don't let situations get out of control and threaten your motivation to homeschool. Prevention is the key to handling sibling rivalry.

Train your children from an early age to respect others, share, talk about what bothers them, and control their anger. Set limits and establish clear rules, such as no violence. When the rules get broken, follow through with the consequences so your children will know that you mean what you say. For example, if one child hits another, make eye contact, firmly state that hitting is not allowed, insist that he apologize, and discuss alternatives the child could have used instead of hitting. Finally, administer any repercussions.

If your children squabble a lot, call a family meeting and brainstorm together for solutions to problems while everyone is calm. On your own, look for ways to make life more harmonious in a large household. When children share rooms, designate a secure area for each child's belongings, color-code personal possessions, and find a place where each child can go to be alone. Also, use a timer to prevent anyone from monopolizing the bathroom.

Here are a few more suggestions to prevent sibling rivalry and promote peace:

- **Provide enough toys and activities for different ages.** Blocks, dress-up clothes, and art supplies are good examples. Remove items that cause arguing and buy two of any favorites.
- **Promote family togetherness.** Have family meals and a family read-aloud time. Do devotions together in the morning or before bedtime.
- **Praise children in the act of getting along.** This gives them attention for positive actions.
- **Don't compare your children or show favoritism.** Treat them as individuals. Schedule one-on-one time and go on outings with each one individually so they will be less likely to work for your attention in negative ways.

Don't reward tattletales by over-reacting. However, because your tattler may sometimes tell you something truly important, be sure to listen before you disregard his message. If the situation calls for your intervention, thank him for telling you. Otherwise, acknowledge his feelings and send him back to work out the dispute.

Indeed, encourage your children to work out differences on their own. Monitor the situation and intervene only when the argument appears to be escalating to violence or name-calling. When you do step in, don't take sides, but acknowledge each child's point of view by restating how each one feels. Then help them come up with a solution together. If they are too angry to work together on a solution, separate them. Alternatively, assign extra chores or take away the toy that they are fighting over. One mom in our homeschool group sends her children into each other's rooms to play. This usually encourages them fairly quickly to share!

Most families notice a certain time of day when their children seem to have extra energy and tend to argue most. Sometimes called the "arsenic hour" or "witching hour," this time of day is usually in late afternoon and early evening when parents try to cook supper and spouses arrive home from work. Some parents simply plan for a later supper time and play with their children until their spouses arrive home; then one parent prepares the meal while the other parent plays with the kids. If this is not an option for you, try these tactics:

- Take everyone outside to run around the yard or walk around the block.
- Include your kids in supper preparations.
- Designate this time for afternoon chores to keep them busy.
- Send them to their rooms for alone time to read or play quietly.
- Make this period of the day the read-aloud time or bath time to calm them down.

- Put on an educational video or DVD.
- Prepare a box of special toys, books on tape, board games, and quiet electronic games that are used only at this time.

Squabbling children will wear down your motivation to continue homeschooling. However, if you are prepared for your children's behavior, you will be able to control the situation and maintain discipline.

Discipline

Discipline and obedience are important in any family, but particularly in a homeschooling family of more than one child. For homeschooling to work effectively, your children must obey you. To get them to obey, you must be consistent both in expectations and in any consequences of disobedience. Each and every time you must follow through so your children will know that you mean what you say. Start training your children as babies. Set limits. Require obedience even in small, unimportant matters, so when they are older they will already have learned that you mean what you say, and they will obey. It is not too late for older children, but be prepared for a lot of repetition that could have been avoided if you had started when they were young.

Of course, you can always refer continuing discipline matters to the "principal"—in most cases, Dad. The two of you together present a united front, so have your spouse give a pep talk to the children, explaining how important school is, how they must obey their teacher, and what the repercussions will be if they continue being uncooperative. After all, life is filled with responsibilities we may not like but must do anyway, and all our actions have consequences.

Rewards and Consequences

Consider instituting concrete rewards and consequences, but use your discretion in this matter. Some families do not advocate rewards and punishments, preferring children to want to learn for learning's sake. However, children should understand not only the results of diligence and hard work but also the consequences of irresponsibility and laziness.

Consequences do not have to be elaborate. One mom in our homeschool group has a simple penalty for complaining or whining. Every time one of her children complains, he must sit with his hands over his mouth for one full minute. Another mom assigns copy work in the form of sentences such as "I will obey my mother." Incidentally, after years of copy work, her sons now have beautiful penmanship!

Here are more ideas that other families have used as penalties, depending on the ages of the children:

- Loss of privileges, such as no computer, no television, no stereo, no video games, and no car
- Restriction from friends
- Grounding them to the house for a period of time
- Restriction to their room until they apologize
- Early bedtime
- Extra page of school work
- Monetary fine, such as a nickel for an inappropriate tone of voice
- Extra chores, such as weeding the flower beds or cleaning out the refrigerator

One family in our homeschool group uses the "tomato staking" method explained by Elizabeth Krueger, homeschooling mother of 10 and founder of www.ATripToTheWoodshed.com. Basically, the disobedient child is kept close to you so you can watch and correct his misbehavior immediately. He stays by you as you go about your household duties until you trust him enough to behave on his own. Some families reverse this technique and stay by the offending child instead. Either method works because the child does not like the fact that his parent cannot trust his behavior without being beside him.

Good behavior includes obeying with a cheerful attitude. A positive attitude is important, from you and the children. Just one complaining person can bring down the whole group. Therefore, make it clear that whining and complaining lead to extra chores. Then make the chores hot, tiring and no fun at all.

To help keep a positive attitude, praise your children when they have earned it, and do not compare them to each other. All children are different, with different strengths as well as different weaknesses. Unfair comparisons produce negative results, so praise their individual diligence, hard work, and progress. Elizabeth Krueger cautions not to go overboard with praise for every little deed, however. Children will likely see through the flattery and eventually not believe your sincere compliments. Also, don't praise them for attributes they have no control over, such as their looks or intelligence. Instead, commend them for doing well, such as when they try hard or do more than you expect.

In addition to praise, reward good behavior and diligent work with extra time with friends, a lunch out with mom or dad, a later bedtime or an extra story at story time. As with these suggestions, the best rewards involve quality time with a parent or friend. Occasionally, however, you may want to acknowledge a hard-working student with a tangible reward, such as the new bow your archer has been wanting or the book your avid reader wants.

Special One-on-One Time

The individual one-on-one nature of homeschooling motivates students to do their best and helps prevent sibling rivalry. When each one of my children started "school," we had quality time together every day. The preschooler and baby received special attention because I read to them, rocked them, and played with them a little every day. Now that three of my children study independently, I can devote one-on-one time to my youngest child as she learns to read.

Besides focused school time, plan special activities and outings for each child. Depending on how many children you have and the free time you and your husband have, you could set aside a few hours each week or plan a whole day each weekend or once a month. If you have to, mark the special day on the calendar so you will not forget. Pastimes do not have to be elaborate, just time together. One mom in our homeschool group assigns each child a different day of the week to help her with dinner. No other child is allowed in the kitchen, and that child is exempt from kitchen duty after dinner. Another mom lets a different child stay up later than the others for quality time together at night once a week.

In our family, Saturday is "Father and Son Day." The two of them play golf, go to the park or just play computer games at home. Then every Tuesday is a lunch date with mom, and I take one child out for lunch anywhere he or she wants to go, except fast food. In addition to "Father and Son Day" and lunch out, my husband and I use errands as special quality time. For example, if my husband needs to go to the store, he will take one of our children along and leave the others at home with me. The one on the errand enjoys special time alone with Dad, and the ones at home enjoy time at home without that one sibling.

Getting Your Students' Best Work

If you have problems with a student's attitude or performance, evaluate the situation. Answer the following questions:

- Could your child have problems with his sight or hearing?
- Are you assigning and planning too much?
- Is the work beyond his level?
- Is there family stress or trauma?

After you have eliminated these problems, you can take a different approach. Clearly explain from the beginning how you will evaluate school work. Then your students will know what is expected of them and they can focus on meeting and exceeding your expectations. For those who are lazy, send back any work that is less than acceptable for them to do again. A few days of having to redo all their work will likely make them do their best from the beginning. This has definitely succeeded with our children.

One family in our support group uses their children's allowance as an incentive to work hard. As being a good student is each child's "job," each one is required to do school work and chores efficiently. Failure to do so results in docked "pay." After initiation of this new policy, their children have shown marked improvements in academic performance and attitude.

Showcasing your students' work may also improve their performance and motivate them to do their best. Post excellent worksheets and research papers on the refrigerator for everyone to admire. We use our refrigerator in addition to a large corkboard. Some families prepare an end-of-unit or end-of-year presentation for friends and relatives. We invite grandparents for our end-of-year celebrations, but Victoria's family invites relatives and family friends for a cook-out. Her seven children recite Scripture passages, give musical recitals, and present their latest projects.

Alternatively, you may want to put together a portfolio or scrapbook of the school year to show relatives and guests, even if your state does not require one. Most likely, your children will not want to display inferior work, and they will be motivated to do their best.

One mom in our homeschool group has found a daily routine that motivates her small children. She goes over the high and low moments that happen each day as she tucks them into bed at night and discusses how she and they could improve for tomorrow. She asks them if they are doing their best, if they would be proud to show their work to someone else, and if they think God would be pleased with their efforts.

Indeed, perhaps the best incentive for your children and motivation for you will be the knowledge that God has a unique plan for their lives and that their education prepares them for it. This will give a new importance and purpose to their education, and their motivation for learning will be to please God, not just their parents. This has really motivated our children to focus on their individual talents, improve their skills, and do their best.

Motivating Teenagers

Junior high and high school students may seem harder to motivate and discipline than younger students. After all, they are young adults, and you cannot *make* them learn; however, you can decide on proper conduct and follow through with the consequences of disobedience. If you resort to grounding, for instance, stick with it until you see a change, no matter how long it takes.

Place responsibility for older children's education on them. They will appreciate the trust. Tell junior high students that the school year ends when these books have been read and these assignments have been completed. Show high school students the schedule of credits they must earn to graduate. Either they can work diligently and finish in a timely manner, or they can dawdle and still be working when their friends and siblings are finished and taking a break. Some families place the education of teenaged sons under their father's direct guidance. Victoria, homeschooling mother of seven, has found this method successful with her sons.

Another option may be to enroll your teenagers in a co-op class. Knowing they must share with others in the class provides both motivation and accountability. For parents who feel their teenagers do not take them seriously as teachers, a co-op may be the answer.

If your teenager neglects his studies and you know he can do better, try to find the underlying reason for his attitude. Give him a chance to explain. As a young adult, he should be able to express himself fairly well. He may have some valid points; perhaps he does not like the curriculum, or maybe he does not see "the point" in it all.

If he does not like the curriculum, allow him to design his own plan of study. He just may get excited about school again! Not only will he learn this way, but also he will learn how to learn and how to use what he learns. To provide accountability, schedule deadlines for completing various goals he has set and periodic "checkups" to ensure he stays on track. Alternatively, ask a friend or relative to serve as his accountability partner. Having an outsider, such as a pastor or sports coach, hold him responsible for his work may relieve some of the tension between you and your teen.

If he does not see the point of his education, try an apprenticeship class. One mom in our homeschool group found this method successful with her son. What you do is have him list three or four careers he is interested in, then have him spend two weeks on each career. Part of the process would include researching each career field, interviewing someone in that position, arranging a field day to get an idea of what that person actually does, and writing a report on why he would pursue this career or not. If he questions the reason for his education, this project will illustrate why education is important to achieve his goals. Plus, it may help him establish a career goal and inspire him to reach it.

On the other hand, if you feel your teenager is just lazy and self-serving, then cut out school for two or three weeks and have him volunteer to read to the elderly at a nursing home, deliver food to the homebound, or help build a home for Habitat for Humanity. One mother in our homeschool group found that getting her son to serve others in some way not only brought about the necessary attitude adjustment but also significantly reduced the stress in their family.

Vacations

Vacations reduce stress and promote family togetherness, so save up for that annual family vacation. Traveling and going on vacations offer unique opportunities to learn geography and history, play car games, and read maps. Before your trip, research the local history and get brochures from the chamber of commerce. When you arrive at your destination, explore the area. These excursions add spice to your children's education and provide a well-deserved break.

If vacations are financially unfeasible, take several "mini" vacations throughout the year. Go on day trips up to three hours from home. Go on family outings, such as on a picnic, to the movies or to a restaurant. One restaurant near us lets children younger than 12 years old eat free; as a result, we eat there at least once a month. For a while, all four of our children ate for free!

Experiment with a "home vacation" by staying home on a weekend, turning off the phone, and planning fun foods and activities together as a family. If you have extra money, consider ordering pizza delivery, eating out for one meal, or going to a family movie. One family in our homeschool group simply goes camping in their back yard for the weekend.

Regular Breaks

Even if you do not go on vacations, at least take a few long breaks. School breaks help students and parents stay motivated throughout the year. Some families homeschool year-round so they can enjoy long vacations scattered throughout the year. With a year-round schedule, you can easily take off a week for major and minor holidays, or even an entire month for Christmas. Other families alternate two, four or six weeks of school followed by one week off. A full week off may motivate your children to work diligently for a few weeks.

Another advantage to homeschooling year-round is the ability to accommodate unexpected illnesses and emergencies. You will not become frustrated if you fall behind schedule because you will be able to make up the time easily. Plus, with a year-round schedule your children will not lose what they have learned between long summer breaks, and you will not have to spend four to six weeks in the fall reviewing old material.

In addition to regular breaks and vacations, give yourself a break each week by instituting a four-day school week. As an incentive to take Friday off, everyone needs to complete school work on the other days of the week. Alternatively, Fridays could be set aside for field trips, special projects, or family day. One family I know reserves Friday night as family night. They order pizza, picnic in the living room, pop popcorn, and watch a video. Playing games together is another easy way to relax and bond with your children.

You and your children need daily breaks, too. Perhaps give them a short break after every two subjects; ten minutes should be sufficient. Also, institute a "quiet time" every day. This is mandatory time in the afternoon when all children retire to separate rooms to nap, play quietly, read, or work on a project, depending on their ages. You can use the time to rest, read or pursue a hobby. Not only will you benefit from an afternoon break, but also your children will enjoy their time together the rest of the day even more. We have always had quiet time in our family, and even the children appreciate the respite.

No matter what, take a break from school whenever you feel stressed. Retreat to the backyard and relax in a hammock; hang up wind chimes and plant flowers near your backyard retreat. Too cold to go out? Curl up in a comfy chair with a hot drink, read a good book or look through your photo albums. If necessary, take a couple of days off and evaluate what is stressing you. Sometimes just a little break will reduce stress and make a big difference in your attitude.

Creative Outlets and Diversions

When you and your children need a break, indulge in creative outlets. A few minutes diverted from your regular routine can refresh and revitalize you. Pam credits creative outlets for preventing burnout in her family. One of her daughters cooks to relax while another plays the piano and Pam herself pulls weeds and plants flowers. Your children may prefer other diversions, such as reading, running, listening to music, or painting.

Other excellent creative outlets include extracurricular activities, hobbies, and competitions. Art, music, gymnastics, dance, scouts, and sports provide a nice balance to school work. Many homeschool groups and umbrella schools offer clubs and athletics. An interesting hobby will motivate your children to learn more about it, and working hard to prepare for a contest or complete a project spreads the excitement and energy to other areas. Plus, simply having a specific goal in mind provides motivation for some children.

However, do not fill your spare time with too many outside pursuits. As Anita does with her four kids, limit your children's extracurricular activities to one or two per child. With more than one child, you will have difficulty staying energized for school if you are juggling ball practice, dance class, gymnastics, and scouts in addition to school and housework. Students will burn out, too, due to an overextended schedule. Plus, being on the go too much will upset the routines of very small children, making them cranky.

Friends are important diversions, too. Give your kids time with their pals without siblings tagging along. Let them go to friends' houses and invite friends over. If their friends go to traditional school, get a copy of the school calendar and plan playdates for school holidays. However, homeschoolers need to make friends with other homeschoolers. If your children's friends go to traditional schools, your children may feel left out, even if they like homeschooling. To alleviate this problem, join a homeschool support group where they can make friends who homeschool.

Use free time with friends as an incentive to get work done. Make a rule that no one can come over each day until all school work and chores are done. Remind your dawdling student that he can waste time all he wants, but he only delays and shortens his time with friends because they cannot come over until he has finished.

This rule may also apply to the television and computer. Use favorite television programs and computer time as incentives to complete school work in a reasonable time. One mom in our homeschool group does not allow the television to be turned on at all until her children have completed their morning chores, breakfast, and school work. Even then, they are limited to one show. Indeed, limit both television and computer time. We use a token system for the computer whereby each child gets four tokens, each worth 15 minutes. They earn extra tokens for the computer by doing extra chores.

Internet Groups

The computer may provide the support and motivation parents need through an online homeschool discussion group. You can join email groups for large families, specific states or regions, and certain curricula. Sometimes members who live near each other make plans for field trips and other activities offline. Go to www.Groups.Yahoo.com or www.Groups.MSN.com and search for an email group using your hometown, area cities, and "homeschool" as keywords.

For families who live far from metropolitan areas, the Internet bridges the miles between a homeschooling family in a large city on the Eastern seaboard and another family on a farm in the Midwest. Because the Internet is accessible 24/7, you can find encouragement and advice whenever you feel stressed and over-whelmed.

Marriage and Homeschooling

Your best source for encouragement and help may be your spouse. Share your homeschool triumphs and concerns with him, solve problems and celebrate milestones together. With several children needing your attention and time, your marriage can easily fall by the wayside, but that relationship is important to provide the support you need to handle several children.

Your husband can cheer you in your homeschooling efforts at any time, but time away together can provide that extra boost for school. Get a sitter so you two can meet for lunch or go out occasionally. If going out to dinner or a movie is financially unfeasible, institute an age-appropriate bedtime for your children and stick to it. This allows the two of you to have time for yourselves after the children are in bed. Another option may be to have a set time early in the evening when you and your spouse retire to your bedroom and children are not allowed to interrupt, except for emergencies. If you and your husband are morning people, get up an hour before your children and share breakfast or coffee together. In any case, do not neglect the strength that can come from your marriage.

Your husband can also provide assistance in practical ways. He can teach a subject that he knows better than you, correct school work each day, read aloud at bedtime, drive students to their extracurricular engagements, and include the children in his hobbies and projects. Victoria actually turns over her teenage sons to their father's direct influence and discipline. Just as your daughters have a female role model and authority figure in you, your sons need a male role model and authority figure in their father. Besides, it is important for children to get to know their dad and for him to get to know them. Not to mention, his involvement in homeschooling lessens the burden on you and keeps your enthusiasm up.

Preventing Teacher Burnout

Feeling stressed, overwhelmed, and under-supported often leads to burnout. This can occur during an especially busy year or after homeschooling several years in a row. The best solution is prevention, and this section deals specifically with additional measures you can take to prevent homeschool burnout.

Set your priorities. When matters get pressing, Victoria, mother of seven, reminds herself of her priorities as a Christian first, wife second, mother third, and teacher next. Your concerns may be different, but once you have set your priorities, learn to say no to additional commitments. Perhaps limit outside obligations to one main area. You can become more involved in your church and community once you have fewer children who need you at home.

Once your teenagers can drive, let them know that they will sometimes be asked to chauffeur siblings, get groceries, and run errands. Your teens can also assist you in other ways as needed. As your administrative assistants, they can take messages, babysit the little ones, write grocery lists, settle minor arguments, sort the mail, and do the bills each month. As teacher's aides, they can read to their siblings, answer questions, correct school work, and help with scheduling. If you have some assistance, you will not feel so frazzled.

Many times we become so busy that we neglect ourselves, which only sets us up for burnout. Get plenty of sleep and make time for yourself. Use your children's independent study time or daily quiet time to get your mind off school. Exercise, do devotions, read, or go for a walk. Pam, mother of three, spends time outside in her flower beds, and Victoria, mother of seven, turns to her friends in person or by phone or email.

Pursue your interests. Be an example of life-long learning and take a class or learn to play a musical instrument. Join a Bible study group or book club. I participate in a ladies' Christian book club where I get a chance to spend time with other like-minded adults and discuss good books each week. Plus, I enjoy the regular break from home responsibilities, and my children enjoy a day off from school! Breaks like this can certainly relieve stress and re-energize you.

Perhaps the best stress-reliever is regular exercise. Exercise keeps you healthy and helps you lose weight and maintain a healthy weight. Your children need to see you exercising so that they, too, will learn healthy habits. If you cannot exercise with kids underfoot, work out before they awake in the morning, after they go to bed, or during quiet time. Invest in a work out tape, join a gym with a nursery, start a walking or aerobics group with other parents, or load the kids in a stroller and on bikes and walk around the neighborhood for 30 minutes. You will be amazed at the extra energy you will have after just a couple of weeks of an exercise routine.

Here are a few more suggestions to help you prevent burnout:

- **Attend homeschool conferences and workshops.** Many groups organize special speakers and seminars that can be very inspirational and insightful. Take your husband along with you; his enthusiasm will inspire you, too.
- **Read homeschool magazines and books.** They will inspire and encourage you. Plus, you may learn valuable tips from education professionals and other homeschooling families.

- **Participate in a homeschool support group.** If one does not meet near you, arrange activities with other families or friends, such as an afternoon tea or moms' night out. Share your experiences with other parents and seek their advice.
- **Turn to your relatives, friends, and church family.** Give your children weekends alone with grandma now and then, and sign them up for occasional church activities.
- **Start each school year slowly.** Start with one or two subjects and gradually add more over several weeks. This will help all of you adjust to a new routine and prevent burnout.
- **Pray and trust God.** When things seem overwhelming or stressful, take your concerns to the Lord in prayer. Go to Him for guidance, wisdom, and strength, and He will not fail you.

Chapter 14

Socialization: Finding Something for Everyone

Through a homeschool support group, students participate in co-ops, clubs and sports.

The increasing popularity of home education over the years has made the socialization issue much easier to address and eliminate. Homeschoolers organize field trips with other families and get involved in support groups, communities, and churches. They also participate in extracurricular activities, such as clubs and sports, where they spend quality time with their peers. As a result, you and your children will not be isolated at home; you will find numerous socialization opportunities for all of your children if you just look around you and take advantage of what you discover.

Homeschool Support Groups

You will not likely find anything that offers so much for all your children at one time as a homeschool support group. Groups offer both playtime and structured activities that appeal to a wide range of ages. In fact, most homeschoolers rely on support groups as their primary means for socialization for their preschoolers, adolescents, preteens, and teenagers.

Kids of all ages will enjoy field trips, science fairs, monthly parties, and other special events sponsored by homeschool groups. They will have an opportunity to participate in clubs, sports, co-ops, and service projects. Members get a chance to see the local sites and learn more about the community. Some support groups even publish a yearbook, organize a prom, and plan a senior trip. If your group does not offer what your children want, spearhead efforts to start it and get other parents and children involved. Our homeschool group publishes a yearbook because I wanted my children to have one. Similarly, another homeschool group now hosts a homeschool prom because the teenage daughters of one of the members desired one. If you and your children are interested in a new club or activity, most likely others will be, too.

Homeschool support groups are not just for children; parents will find many reasons to justify participating in a group. All parents need a break now and then, but many do not have the extra money to spend on babysitters or on going out. Homeschool groups offer the opportunity for parents to get a regular break from home and to spend time with their children at the same time. During that therapeutic break, parents can seek advice and share experiences. Members vary from those who have homeschooled for many years to those who have just started. As a result, parents learn practical homeschool tips and keep abreast of local laws.

Additionally, many support groups sponsor homeschool conferences, conventions, and seminars featuring special guest speakers who motivate and inspire participants. Some groups host curriculum fairs, providing members with an opportunity to buy and sell used books or to examine and order curricula directly from attending vendors.

Most homeschool groups also provide valuable assistance during times of personal need and family emergencies. Since many families these days do not have relatives nearby, their local homeschool group provides that missing element of support. Indeed, many parents find it convenient and comforting to have someone they can call for a quick babysitting duty in an emergency; through the group, their children know and feel comfortable with that other adult or teenager as well.

On a related note, homeschooled teenagers make wonderful babysitters! They often have experience with small children through their involvement with a homeschool group, and they are usually available during the day when other teens are in school. Our family has always employed homeschoolers, and now our oldest daughter babysits for other families.

Incidentally, involvement in a homeschool support group may provide financial benefits to members. Many area businesses offer discounts to groups. Support groups organize barter systems for members to exchange goods, such as coupons and children's clothes, and services, such as mowing the lawn, painting a room, and sewing clothes.

Now that you realize the value of participating in a support group, search for one near you. If there are several groups in your area, visit each of them. You may feel more comfortable and have more in common with the members of one group over another. On the other hand, if you like them all, join them all! Try these methods to find a group near you:

- **Ask your umbrella school.** The administrators should have information on any local groups.
- **Contact local churches, libraries, and YMCAs.** Many support groups meet in these locations, or the employees may know of a local group.
- **Go online.** Web sites such as www.HSLDA.org and www.NHEN.org maintain directories of support groups. Also, you can use a search engine by using your city, state, and "homeschool support group" as keywords.
- **Check the community calendar of the newspaper.** Many groups advertise their meetings.
- **Glance over community bulletin boards.** Groups often post fliers in libraries, bookstores, parks, playgrounds, churches, and businesses where homeschoolers shop.
- **Go to the local park or playground on Fridays.** Homeschoolers usually meet at parks and libraries regularly on Fridays. You may bump into a group while you are there!
- **Ask around among your friends.** If you already know a few homeschoolers, they may be able to direct you to an organization. If not, ask parents with school-aged children that you see during the day if they homeschool. Since their children are not in school, they may homeschool and may know about a local group.

Co-ops

Joining a co-op through a local homeschool group provides social as well as academic and financial benefits. Co-ops are often designed for children of similar ages and interests, so students have a chance to spend time with their peers learning various subjects together. Participants learn teamwork as well as discussion and debate skills. In addition, families share the cost of expensive materials, such as science equipment. A co-op may provide parents with the best opportunity to teach difficult subjects, such as Latin and chemistry, or group subjects, such as drama and P.E. Sometimes a few families get together to co-op the same packaged curriculum; they share lessons, exhibit projects, and go on field trips together.

While parents may lose some overall control in a co-op, they gain other benefits. The parents involved either split the courses according to their individual skills or engage an "expert," so they know that their children are taught by someone knowledgeable in that particular subject. Their children have a chance to improve in areas where they need help and excel in areas where they show promise. Parents also appreciate the accountability and objective audience inherent in the co-op classroom environment. Because students will be expected to share with others in the co-op, they will be motivated to do their best work. Plus, children who feel their parents praise their work even when undeserved will find an objective audience for their writing, research, and projects.

Find out if your local homeschool group offers co-ops. If not, consider starting one. As with other activities offered through the group, if your children want to start a new co-op to learn more about a particular subject, most likely others will, too.

Field Trips

Field trips through a homeschool group or field trip club provide both socialization and education opportunities. Historic locations and living history days make history come alive for children. Many cities boast children's museums and science museums with fun, hands-on learning activities. You can even turn a vacation into a social and learning experience by visiting area museums and historic sites in addition to the usual amusement parks. In fact, many amusement parks, museums, and zoos host a "Homeschool Day" with special activities and discounted admission, which will be helpful for a large family on a budget. Check with the facility near you and with your local homeschool group. Additionally, search the Internet for "homeschool day."

However, you are not limited to museums, historic sites, and festivals that charge entrance fees. Large families or those on a limited budget may not be able to afford admission for several children. Therefore, peruse family magazines and consult the chamber of commerce, parks department, newspaper, and yellow pages for free locations. Then call the location to set up a tour. Many businesses accommodate tours for free, and finding out how chocolate is made in the local sweet shop and how the grocery store gets supplies make fascinating learning experiences. A trip to an "ordinary" place teaches children to observe and ask questions. Be sure to include sites in neighboring cities and short day trips to the beach or mountains.

No matter where you decide to go, you may not always be able to find locations that accommodate the ages and interests of all your children at once. To alleviate the problem somewhat, encourage your children to suggest field trips. If you plan the trips on your own, keep your children's interests in mind, choose places that cater to their ages and grade levels as much as possible, and be prepared to explain information that may be beyond the understanding of small children.

Here are a few more suggestions to accommodate all ages:

- Plan trips for weekends when your spouse can help out.
- Ask a homeschool teenager, grandparents or other relatives to come along to lend a hand.
- Invite another parent and her children to go with your family.
- Solicit a neighbor, relative or sitter to look after one or two children at home.
- Let teenagers stay home if they are not interested in a tour designed for their siblings.
- Use a network of friends to trade babysitting favors and rides.
- Allow your children to bring a friend along to make the trip more fun.

Despite all your efforts, occasionally some of your children will have no choice but to tag along for the ride. If so, remind them that you expect a cheerful attitude because they got to choose previous field trips and will likely get a chance to choose again soon.

The tour will go much more smoothly if you prepare in advance. Unless you have adults along to help, avoid large crowds and keep your group small. If you have babies or toddlers, find out if strollers are allowed. If so, use them! Also, if you request a tour guide, specify the length of the tour. As we have learned from our homeschool group, the younger the children, the shorter the speaking portion of the tour should last!

On the day of the event, pack snacks, drinks, baby supplies if necessary, and a camera. To avoid confusion, your kids should wear bright colors so you can spot them easily in a crowd or at a distance. When arriving and leaving, do a count or roll call to ensure that you have not forgotten anyone. To prevent potential problems, tell the children in advance what is expected of them and what behavior is unacceptable. Even common sense rules bear repeating, so remind them to stay with you, listen to the tour guide, use good manners, and refrain from yelling and running.

Of course, adults have rules, too. Keep an eye on your children at all times, and do not expect older children to watch their siblings. Also, remove any disruptive children. Be sure to follow any rules the host may have as well. After all, field trip hosts do not have to provide educational opportunities for your children. Their choice to do so may well be influenced by your behavior.

Sports

Many homeschoolers rely on sports for socialization and recreation. As a result, large support groups and umbrella schools often provide their members with various athletic programs, including soccer, baseball, basketball, volleyball, football, golf, and track. For information on homeschool sports teams in your area, go to the Home School Sports Network at www.HSPN.net and National Christian Homeschool Athletic Association at www.geocities.com/nchaasports/.

However, your children are not limited to homeschool sports. Many homeschoolers participate in the same after-school athletic programs available to public and private schooled students through YMCAs, community centers, and city recreation departments. In addition, churches sponsor Upward sports ministries in basketball, soccer, and cheerleading. Go to www.upward.com to find a league near you. Businesses affiliated with sports offer additional options for homeschoolers, so contact local golf courses, ski shops, martial arts centers, and archery supply shops for information on classes.

Extracurricular Activities

Pam, a homeschooling mom of three, calls socialization a "by-product" of extracurricular pursuits, such as city softball, YMCA basketball, homeschool bowling, group musical instrument lessons, and summer camps, because socialization is not the primary aim. Children need sports for physical activity and music to round out their educational experiences, and many of these are available for all ages. As Pam has done, enroll your own children in extracurricular activities and benefit from the socialization by-product.

Here are a few more suggestions for extracurricular activities for all ages:

- **Music, dance, and art lessons are often provided through the community.** Ask around, and check the newspaper and yellow pages.

- **You can find special classes for toddlers and preschoolers, too.** Consider a preschool dance class, a Mom's Day Out program at a church, a mommy and me class at the community center, and a preschool gymnastics class at the YMCA.
- **Your children may enjoy 4-H, scouts, and Keepers of the Faith.** These organizations may even have homeschool chapters. Ask around or contact the organization's headquarters.
- **Adult civic organizations and clubs are open to teenagers.** Organizations such as Civil Air Patrol, Toastmasters, and the local computer users group extend membership to teenagers.
- **Your children could join the homeschool band, community orchestra, youth choir or theatre group.** Ask around for more information or check the yellow pages.

Playgroups

While your older children are involved in various extracurricular activities, your toddlers and preschoolers will enjoy playing with kids their age in a playgroup. Playgroups are usually designed for infants, toddlers, preschoolers, and their at-home moms, whether they homeschool or not. In most playgroups, children play together while parents talk. During play, youngsters learn valuable social skills, such as how to share, take turns, and role-play. Some playgroups feature field trips, crafts, and structured activities that reinforce skills the children may be learning at home.

Regardless of activities, the key benefits of a playgroup are the opportunities for socializing and making friends for both parents and young children. I started my first playgroup when my oldest child was four years old, and I stayed with the group until my fourth child turned five years old nearly 10 years later. As a result, all four of my children made their first friends in playgroup, and we are still friends with many of them today.

You can search the Internet for a playgroup, moms' club, and parents' organization near you by using those keywords along with the name of your hometown and state. Additionally, check the directories at www.OnlinePlaygroup.com and www.MommyAndMe.com. Also, contact local churches and community centers where groups are likely to meet, and check the community calendar of the newspaper for meeting announcements.

Church

Involve your children in activities at your house of worship. Sunday school offers a chance to meet peers on a regular basis. Don't forget about other church-sponsored programs, such as Bible studies, choirs, Vacation Bible School, outreach ministries, missionary opportunities, special retreats, and youth group activities. Some churches host Awana programs and Pioneer Clubs and sponsor Upward sports ministries. Large churches may even offer special classes; one of our daughters has enjoyed a unique opportunity to learn puppetry through our church. If your church gears programs mostly to young children, your preteens and teenagers could volunteer to teach or lead a group.

Rather than go to church, some homeschoolers choose to home fellowship with a few other like-minded families. Victoria and her family of seven children enjoy this type of fellowship with three other families. Each family takes a turn hosting the group, with the host father leading and family members participating in worship. Older children plan outreach activities and help with little ones. Whether you organize family services or join a church, reach out to others of your faith for appropriate social opportunities.

Neighborhood and Community

You can find many social opportunities in your neighborhood and community. Make an effort to meet your neighbors and invite those with children to come over in the afternoons or join you at the park. Also, attend community events, festivals, and parades.

Find out what your community has to offer for recreation by checking the chamber of commerce, newspaper, and yellow pages. Even small towns may have a skating rink, bowling alley or children's museum where your children can meet other kids. Most libraries and bookstores offer free story time activities weekly. This is a great way to meet other preschoolers and their parents.

Volunteer in your community through your homeschool support group, cover school, and church. Actually, you and your children can volunteer in various ways on your own. Organize a fundraiser for a local charity or decorate a retirement home for the holidays. You could also visit the elderly, collect your children's outgrown clothing for a local outreach program, deliver toys to a homeless shelter, and volunteer to distribute meals to the homebound. Organize a weekly story hour at the library; all of your children could help with the theme, stories, and crafts. The animal shelter and food bank may appreciate regular help in some way, too.

By volunteering for a local agency or organizing a community service project, not only would you be serving your community, but also your children would benefit from participating in your efforts. Your actions will go a long way in teaching them the importance of community service and the satisfaction of helping others.

Friends

Friends are an integral part of socialization for children of all ages. It will take some effort on your part, and each child's, to make and keep friends. After all, public schooled children are confined with other kids their own age for several hours a week, so they have the peers and ample time to develop friendships, even if the only thing they have in common is that they sit beside each other in math class. Making friends is fairly easy in such a restricted environment. On the other hand, while a homeschooler must actively seek time with friends because they are not thrown together by circumstances every weekday, he has the advantage of choosing friends from among peers who share his interests.

To facilitate friendships, try these suggestions:

- Seek families with children of similar ages in homeschool support groups, clubs, and other organizations.
- Meet the parents of your children's new friends.
- Invite children over to play or hang out, with or without their parents.
- Have fun, age-appropriate activities so they will want to come over.
- Invite your children's friends to go along on your next field trip.
- Plan social activities, such as excursions to the park, sleepovers, camping out, or an afternoon of skating or bowling.

Schedule activities on a regular basis. My second daughter's best friend lives only two miles down the road, so the two of them spend a lot of time together. On the other hand, my oldest daughter and her friend have such busy schedules that sometimes they go nearly two weeks without seeing each other. Her mother and I finally devised a plan whereby her daughter comes over to our house every Monday afternoon and my daughter goes to their house every Friday afternoon. Of course, sometimes either one of us may have to cancel, but basically, Monday and Friday hold from week to week.

I have made a similar arrangement with the mother of my son's friend. We get together with our sons once a week, and each week we set a date for the following week. Although the days may change depending on our schedules, we still get together weekly for them to play and for us to talk. It does not matter what kind of plan you devise, as long as your children get to spend regular time with their friends.

In addition to providing time with peers, teach your children the characteristics of a good friend. Don't assume that your children know how to pick good friends, and this goes for all children, whether homeschooled or not. They may not understand how a friend's bad trait can influence their own behavior and attitude. Help your children search for friends who are uplifting, honest, and understanding, and teach them to be good friends in return. After all, your children's friends will have nearly as much of an influence on the kind of person they become as you will.

Additional Socialization Opportunities

As homeschoolers, your children will have socialization opportunities unavailable to public and private schooled children. Because your children have a flexible schedule that offers free time during the day, they can socialize at any time and any place.

Turn your errands into socialization opportunities. Because your children are not confined to a classroom all day with 20 other children, they can learn social skills in real life situations. Model good social skills for your children because they will watch your interactions with others. Let them see how you meet strangers, how you treat friends, how you settle conflicts, and how you handle various social situations. Praise their social skills in action and, if necessary, explain in advance how to act in certain circumstances. When you are not in a hurry and there is not a line behind you, let your children satisfy their curiosity about the post office employee or grocery store cashier by asking questions about their work and equipment. Going to the dentist, picking up the dry cleaning and getting the oil changed in the car are all examples of social and educational opportunities.

Go to the park or playground frequently. If you have small children, occasionally go to a fast food restaurant that has a playland. Your youngsters will definitely meet other children at all of these locations. Some may be just playmates for an hour, while others may turn into long-lasting friends. If you go on a Friday, you may meet other homeschoolers because many of them designate Friday as park day.

Don't forget family. Pam and her family make their relatives their primary social circle. As a result, some very special relationships have flourished between generations and among family members that would not have formed under other circumstances. As Pam's family illustrates, one of the benefits of homeschooling is the chance to nurture family relationships.

Conclusion

You can homeschool more than one child successfully!

You can do it! You can homeschool more than one child successfully! If I can do it, and Victoria, Pam, Anita, and all the other homeschooling moms who have contributed in one way or another to this book can do it, then you can do it, too! Your methods may be different from ours; indeed, they probably will be, but they will be no less valuable and successful.

How do you homeschool more than one child successfully? I have spent the bulk of this book answering that question with information from extensive research, advice from my homeschooling friends, and practical tips from my own experiences. You should be able to take these tips and suggestions and apply them to your own family, using what works for you, discarding a few, and modifying others to adapt them to your unique situation.

Now that you have reached the end of this book, you may wonder, "What would you tell a homeschooler who has more than one child that you wish you had known when you first started?" Although the inspirational answers from Victoria, Pam, and Anita may not fit neatly into the practical chapters in this book, they may be just as valuable to homeschoolers of more than one child as all the practical tips will be.

"Good relationships are a foundation stone of a satisfying life," says Victoria, homeschooling mother of seven and grandmother of five. "Knowing my husband more deeply and strengthening that relationship has been a great blessing."

"I wouldn't change using a curriculum centered on our religious beliefs. One's religion and values are more important in the grand scheme of things and are just as important in the academic scheme of things as the three R's," says Pam, homeschooling mom of three. "Also, incorporate a short but regular program of exercise into each school day. Laugh at everything that goes 'wrong.'"

Anita, homeschooling mom of four, says, "Do hands-on creative learning. Read together. Study the Bible together. Learn all day, every day by doing and seeing and talking and living life. Enjoy your family and friends. Enjoy your children; they grow up quickly."

Indeed, they do. As a homeschooler, you are fortunate to be an integral part of your children's lives as they grow up, just as they are fortunate to have you as their parent as well as their teacher.

Bibliography

Personal Interviews

Lofgren, Victoria. Written interview. March 24, 2004.

Olson, Pam. Written interview. March 31, 2004.

Ottinger, Anita. Written interview. March 15, 2004.

Book

Gilbreth, Frank B. and Ernestine Gilbreth Carey. *Cheaper by the Dozen.* New York: Perennial. 2002.

Internet Resources

Arnold, Jody. "Homeschooling with Minimal Academic Structure." Text of a talk at the LIGHT Curriculum Fair. June 1994. <http://members.efn.org/~light/unschool.html> (January 11, 2004).

"Back-to-School Rituals." Counting the Cost. August 2002. <http://www.countingthecost.com/backtoschool.htm> (June 11, 2004).

Berkeley Parents Network: Organizing Kids' Artwork. December 2000. <http://parents.berkeley.edu/advice/household/artwork.html> (July 8, 2004).

Berring, Betty and Vivian Young. "Meeting College Admission Requirements." <http://www.home-school.com/Articles/phs15-berringyoung.html> (June 12, 2004).

Bittner, Terrie. "Secrets of the One Room School: Teaching Multiple Ages." <http://www.geocities.com/athens/oracle/4336/oneroom.html> (January 22, 2004).

Brooks, Lorraine. "Teaching Several Children." <http://www.homeschoolfun.com/?pc_id=2#NEW7> (January 22, 2004).

Campbell, Natasha. "Homeschooling Methods, Part 1." December 2002. <http://www.teach-at-home.com/NCampbell1.asp> (January 19, 2004).

_____. <http://www.teach-at-home.com/NCampbell2.asp> (January 19, 2004).

____. <http://www.teach-at-home.com/NCampbell3.asp> (January 19, 2004).

____. <http://www.teach-at-home.com/NCampbell4.asp> (January 19, 2004).

"Combining Years." Ambleside Online. February 23, 2003. <http://amblesideonline.homestead.com/CombiningYears.html> (January 22, 2004).

Curry, Lorraine. "Combining Work and Homeschool." <http://www.home-school.com/Articles/phs18-lorrainecurry.html> (June 12, 2004).

____. "Homeschooling While Working." Homeschool Zone. <http://www.homeschoolzone.com/hsz/curry.htm#working> (June 12, 2004).

____. "Is Homeschooling Expensive?" Homeschool Zone. <http://www.homeschoolzone.com/hsz/curry.htm#cost> (June 12, 2004).

"Developing a Homeschool Budget." 2004. <http://www.deafhomeschool.com/essentials/gettingstarted/budget.html> (June 12, 2004).

Eaton, Tamara. "Which Method?" <http://www.gocin.com/homeschool/tips-11.htm> (June 12, 2004).

____. "Stress-Free Summer Plans." <http://www.gocin.com/homeschool/week.htm> (June 12, 2004).

____. "Staying on Task." <http://www.gocin.com/homeschool/week48.htm> (June 12, 2004).

____. "Homeschool Management Tips." <http://www.gocin.com/homeschool/tips-1.htm> (June 12, 2004).

____. "Homeschooling with Toddlers." <http://www.gocin.com/homeschool/week29.htm> (June 12, 2004).

____. "Homeschooling Highschoolers." <http://www.gocin.com/homeschool/week10.htm> (June 12, 2004).

____. "Homeschooling in Time of Trials." <http://www.gocin.com/homeschool/week5.htm> (June 12, 2004).

Franklin, Susan. "Design Your Own Preschool Curriculum." October 27, 2000. <http://www.suite101.com/article.cfm/early_learning_at_home/51326> (March 20, 2004).

Hayes, Lenore. "Learning High School Subjects." 2004. <http://www.nhen.org/nhen/pov/teens/default.asp?id=3> (March 20, 2004).

"Helping Siblings To Get Along." HBO & Company. 1998. <http://www.uihealthcare.com/topics/parentingfamilylife/pare4844.html> (December 13, 2004).

Higginbotham, Teresa. "Frugal Homeschool Startup." <http://www.frugalsimplicity.com/article1005.html> (July 31, 2004).

"HomeSchool Tips." <http://homeschool.lifetips.com/Cat.asp__Q__id__E__58651> (December 10, 2004).

"Homeschooling with Notebooks." <http://www.notebooking.org> (January 11, 2004).

"K12 Guide to Teaching More Than One Child." K12 Inc. 2003. <http://www.dswillis.com/pdf/multi_students.pdf> (September 26, 2004).

Krueger, Elizabeth. "The Basics." 2002. <http://www.atriptothewoodshed.com/basic.htm> (June 10, 2004).

____. "Advanced Tomato Staking." 2002. <http://www.atriptothewoodshed.com/advanced_tomato_staking.htm> (June 10, 2004).

Lambert, Steve and Jane Lambert. "One Room School: Teaching Multiple Ages Simultaneously." February 1997. <http://www.fiveinarow.com/support/oneroom.html> (September 26, 2004).

"Learning Styles." <http://www.urbanext.uiuc.edu/succeed/04-learningstyles.html> (March 19, 2004).

Lisenbach, Sherri Perkinson. "Homeschooling When Working Outside the Home." Home School Fun. 2004. <http://www.homeschoolfun.com/default.asp?pc_id=2#NEW15>. (March 20, 2004).

Morris, April. "Homeschooling Methods." 2004.
<http://www.homeschoolingonashoestring.com/homeschooling.html> (January 11, 2004).

Oesterreich, Lesia. "Getting Along: Brothers and Sisters." National Network for Child Care. 1996. <http://www.nncc.org/Parent/ga.brosis.html> (December 10, 2004).

"Plan for College." 2004. <http://www.collegeboard.com/plan> (January 24, 2004).

"Recognizing Home School Diplomas for College Admittance and Financial Aid." Home School Legal Defense Association. September 2002.
<http://www.hslda.org/docs/nche/000001/00000147.asp> (January 24, 2004).

Sanchez, Dionna. "Choosing Friends Wisely." September 21, 2003.
<http://www.onlineplaygroup.com> (January 11, 2004).

Sevy, Bernadine. "Little Ones." 2002.
<http://www.loveathome.com/homeschool/littleones.htm> (March 20, 2004).

Shaw, Isabel. "Leaving School and Learning at Home."
<http://familyeducation.com/article/0,1120,58-26370-0-2,00.html> (March 19, 2004).

Sims, Chris. "Living the Single-Income Lifestyle." National Home Education Network. 2004. <http://www.nhen.org/newhser/default.asp?id=407> (March 20, 2004).

"Single Mom Homeschooling."
<http://www.homeschooloasis.com/art_single_mom_hs.htm> (March 20, 2004).

Storz, Peter. "Dads in Homeschooling: Taking an Active Role." May 2002.
<http://www.homeschoolchristian.com/Features/ActiveDad.html> (June 21, 2004).

"Summer Jobs." 2004.
<http://www.collegeboard.com/parents/article/0,3708,703-704-0-21283,00.html> (June 10, 2004).

Swann, Joyce. "Joyce Swann's Homeschool Tips."
<http://www.home-school.com/Articles/HomeschoolTips.html> (June 12, 2004).

Tanner, Amy. "I Don't Think I Heard You Right! Did You Say Write a Curriculum?" October 1, 2003. <http://www.onlineplaygroup.com> (January 11, 2004).

Tilley-Williams, Carol. "Homeschooling Resources in Your Own Home." PageWise, Inc. 2002. <http://ga.essortment.com/homeschoolingr_rhfq.htm> (January 11, 2004).

"Want Some Ideas for Homeschooling with Toddlers?" Unit Study Helps. 2004. <http://www.unitstudyhelps.com/preschool.htm> (March 20, 2004).

Williams, Lawrence. "Homeschooling with Larger Families." <http://www.oakmeadow.com/resources/articles/large.htm> (January 11, 2004).

Zeise, Ann. "Methods & Styles Directory." <http://homeschooling.gomilpitas.com/methods/Methods.htm> (January 11, 2004).

Index

Achievement Tests, 22

ACT (formerly American College Testing), 73, 75

AP (Advanced Placement), 76

Adolescent, 23, 108

Allowance, 99

Apprenticeship, 73, 77, 100

Arguments, 95, 105

"Arsenic" Hour, 95

Art, 18, 28-29, 53, 70, 74, 95, 102, 112, 122

Assignment Book, 8

Athletics, 8, 19, 69, 102

Attendance, 2, 8

Attention, Keeping Children's, 44, 46, 69

Attitude, 86, 92, 97-102, 111, 116

Baby, 39, 59-60, 62-63, 65, 98, 111

Barter, 31, 65, 109

Bible, 15, 18, 42, 48, 66, 68, 91, 105, 114, 118

Babysitting, 65, 78, 108, 111

Book Lists, 9-10, 21, 39

Bookstores, 16-17, 26-27, 29, 73, 75, 109, 114

Breaks, 52-54, 101-102, 105

Budget, 24-26, 30-31, 35, 110, 120

Bulk Cooking, 88

Burnout, 56, 90, 102, 104-106

Business, 28, 30, 77-78, 80-81

Busy Work, 14, 47, 68, 93

Calendar, 3, 8, 34, 52-54, 59, 91, 98, 103, 109, 113

Carpool, 81, 89

Car School, 59, 89

Character Virtues, 9, 60, 84, 94

Charlotte Mason, 12

Charts, 7, 9, 10, 45, 57, 85, 91

Chores, 5, 56-59, 80, 84-85, 89, 95, 97, 99, 103

Church, 8, 19, 27, 54, 77, 105-106, 113-114

Church Library, 27

Classroom, 17, 22, 37, 56, 68, 110, 116

Classical Teaching Method, 12

Cleaning, 47, 60, 68, 78, 84-86, 88

CLEP (College Level Examination Program), 76

College, 13-14, 22, 45, 49, 54, 73-77, 91, 119, 122

College Admission Tests, 73

Color Coding, 6, 8-10

Community Service, 77, 115

Complaining, 85, 86, 96-97

Compulsory School Age, 2

Computer, 5, 8, 10, 12, 18, 20, 29-30, 34, 37, 39-40, 43, 46, 57, 60, 64, 68-69, 80, 82, 85, 93, 97-98, 103, 113

Conferences, 4, 16, 105, 108

Conflicts, 54, 94, 116

Consequences, 94, 96, 100

Containers, 9, 34, 39, 62, 64, 88

Cooking, 8, 19, 45, 60, 66, 68, 84, 87-88, 95

Co-ops, 18, 49, 75, 107-110

Correspondence Schools, 12, 75

Course of Study, 8, 14, 20-21, 73-74

Crisis, Homeschooling through a, 59-60

Curriculum, Customized, 7, 12, 14, 20-21, 25-26

Curriculum, Designing a, 14, 17, 18-19, 20-21, 25-26

Curriculum, Modifying a, 15

Curriculum, Packaged, 9, 14, 15, 17, 18, 21, 25, 54, 55, 74, 110

Curriculum, Selecting a, 15-17, 25

Curriculum Fairs, 16, 27, 30, 108

Death, 59

Decompression, 5

Diagnostic Tests, 22

Diploma, 2, 75-76

Discipline, 46, 84, 96, 100, 104

Discounts, 27, 109

Distance Learning, 12, 75

Diversions, 102-103

Drama, 18, 43-44, 110

Driver's Education, 18, 74

Dual Enrollment, 76

DVDs, 13, 17

Eclectic, 12

Elementary Grades, 15, 23, 66, 67, 68, 69

Email Groups, 17, 103

Errands, 5, 19, 26, 31, 45, 54-57, 65, 81, 89, 91, 98, 105, 116

Exercise, 44, 65, 93, 105, 118

Expectations, 84, 96, 99

Expenses, 24, 25, 29-31, 34

Extracurricular Activities, 26, 48, 54-56, 59, 79, 91, 102-103, 107, 112-113

Family, 2-4, 7-9, 11-12, 14-15, 18-19, 25-26, 30-31, 35-38, 43, 48-49, 52-54, 56, 58-60, 65, 74, 79, 81-82, 84-89, 91-99, 101-103, 106, 108-111, 114, 116-118

Field Trips, 8-9, 20-21, 23, 27-28, 30, 39, 52, 55, 65-66, 71, 80, 89, 91-93, 102-103, 107-108, 110-111, 113

Fighting, 94-95

Files, 38-39

Focused, Keeping Children, 10, 44, 46-47, 58, 69-70, 91, 99

Foreign Languages, 18, 60

Forms, 7, 9, 28

Forums, 17, 28

Free Resources, 9, 17, 20-21, 22, 25, 27-30, 39, 53, 60, 64, 75, 93,101, 110, 114

Freezer Cooking, 88

Friends, 3, 16, 23, 28, 37, 48, 58, 60, 65, 70-71, 74, 81-82, 84, 89, 91, 97, 99-100, 103, 105-106, 109, 111, 113, 115-118, 122

Games, 8, 12, 17-21, 23, 28, 34, 39, 46, 53, 57, 59-60, 64, 68, 70, 82, 91-92, 94, 96-98, 101-102

GED (General Equivalency Diploma), 75, 76

Goals, 14, 56, 59, 73, 77, 91, 100-101

Grade Level, 12, 15, 20, 26-27, 36, 39, 42-44, 74

Grades, 3, 8-10, 12, 15, 20, 23, 39, 42-43, 66, 76, 80, 93

Grading, 8

Grounding, 97, 100

Health, 7, 19, 105

High School, 2, 7, 10, 14-15, 23, 45, 56, 59, 66, 69, 72-77, 91, 94, 100, 121

History, 12-15, 17-20, 22-23, 25-26, 28, 36, 42, 44, 48, 54, 74, 80, 91, 93, 101, 110

Hobbies, 9, 23, 59, 70, 102, 104

Holidays, 30, 52-54, 101, 103, 114

Home Economics, 19

Home School Legal Defense Association (HSLDA), 2, 3, 75, 76, 109

Home-based Business, 30, 78, 81

Homeschool Conferences, 4, 16, 105, 108

Homeschool Support Group, 3, 6, 29, 71, 103, 106-109, 114
Homework, 5, 47
Housework, 5, 48, 60, 83-86, 89, 103
Husband, see also Spouse, 48-49, 60, 84, 98, 104, 105
Illness, 59
Incentive, 47, 58, 99, 102-103
Independent Learning, 67-68
Independent Study, 14, 45-46, 58, 65, 70, 81, 105
Instructor's Guides, 8, 52
Internet, 4, 13, 17-18, 20-21, 23, 25, 27-29, 35, 39, 50, 53, 64, 72-77, 81, 93, 103, 110, 113, 119
Internet Groups, 103
Internship, 77, 81
Interruptions, 47-48, 58, 59
Journal, 7-8, 38, 59
Junior High School, 7, 10, 56, 69, 72, 73, 100-101
Kindergarten, 23, 68-71
Language Arts, 14-15, 19, 25, 54-55, 57, 76, 80
Laundry, 19, 57-58, 60, 62, 64, 67, 84-87
Laws, 2-3, 18, 74, 78, 80, 108
Learning Environment, 68, 93
Learning Styles, 14, 49-50, 121
Lesson Plans, 7, 9, 13-15, 17-21, 25, 38-39, 54, 93
Library, 2, 4-5, 16-17, 19-20, 23, 25, 27-29, 34, 36, 40, 52, 54, 60, 64, 70, 72, 74-75, 77, 80, 82, 89, 114
Life Skills, 14
Lists, 9-10, 21, 27, 39, 51, 55-56, 85, 89, 91, 94, 105
Literature, 13, 19, 26, 48, 60, 73, 93
Living Books, 93
Marriage, 104

Math, 5, 7, 10, 14-15, 18-19, 23, 25-26, 28, 34, 43, 45-46, 48-49, 53-55, 59, 63, 65-66, 68, 73-74, 76-77, 80, 86, 91, 93, 115
Meals, 19, 31, 47, 57, 60, 79, 81, 84, 87-88, 95, 114
Mentor, 75
Middle School, 56, 69, 94
Military, 59, 77
Missions, 77-78, 114
Motivating Students, 7, 47, 57, 91, 96, 98, 99, 100-101, 103, 110
Motivation, 87, 90, 94, 96, 99-100, 102-103
Multi-Tasking, 57
Music, 8, 19, 47, 53, 57, 68, 81, 85, 87, 93, 102, 112
Nap Time, 62
Newborn, 59
Notebook, 8-9, 34-35, 38, 57
Notebooking, 9, 121
Obedience, 62, 86, 96, 97
Office Supply, 27, 85
One-on-One Instruction, 45, 57, 68, 80
Open Source Software, 29-30
Outings, 53, 65, 95, 98, 101
Packaged Curriculum, 9, 14, 21, 25-27, 54-55, 72, 74, 110
Parks, 18, 109-110
Part time job, 30, 49, 77-78, 80, 81
Party, Back-to-Homeschool, 91
P.E., 19, 110
Physical Education, 19
Playgrounds, 109
Playgroup, 52, 71, 113
Playtime, 23, 35, 47, 59, 60, 62, 63-64, 68, 70, 81, 108, 113
Portfolio, 9, 37-38, 93, 99
Praise, 44, 47, 95, 97, 110, 116
Pregnancy, 59

Preschool, 2, 20, 23, 46, 61-65, 69, 108, 113, 114, 121, 123
Programs, 8, 17-19, 39, 64, 74, 77, 80, 82, 89, 103, 112, 114
Progress Report, 9
Projects, 9, 17, 21, 23, 29, 36-37, 39, 43, 47, 55-58, 62, 68, 76, 80, 91-92, 99, 102, 104, 108, 110
Punishments, 94, 96
Quality Time, 97-98, 107
Quarreling, 94, 105
Quiet Time, 58, 62, 102, 105
Read-Aloud, 5, 13, 43, 44, 47, 58, 60, 63, 70, 93, 95, 104
Reading, 0-1, 5, 8, 12-13, 15, 18, 23, 26, 39, 42, 44-45, 48, 53, 55-59, 65, 68, 70, 74, 80, 93, 102
Records, 6-8, 10
Record-keeping, 7-8, 10, 39
Relatives, 28, 30, 37, 54, 60, 65, 81, 91, 99, 106, 108, 111, 116
Report card, 9
Restriction, 97
Rewards, 20, 85, 96-97
Rules, 94, 112
SAT (formerly Scholastic Aptitude Test), 73, 75
Schedules, 43, 51-54, 56, 59, 72, 94, 115
Scheduling, 45, 51, 53-55, 105
Scholarships, 7, 14, 26, 77, 91
School Room, 37-38, 63
School Time Only Box, 63
Science, 9-10, 13-15, 19, 22-23, 25-26, 29, 33, 36-38, 42, 48-49, 55, 57, 73-74, 76, 91, 93, 108, 110
Scope and Sequence, 9, 13-14, 20-21
Scrapbook, 7, 9, 37, 81, 93, 99
Sibling Rivalry, 94, 98
Single Parents, 79-82

Sports, 19, 23, 26, 34, 48, 65, 100, 102, 107-108, 112, 114
Spouse, 2, 65, 79-80, 96, 104, 111
Social Skills, 113, 116
Socialization, 107-108, 110, 112, 115-116
Software, 12, 17-18, 20, 29-30, 35, 39
State Regulations, 2-3, 18
Storage, 5, 10, 33-34, 36, 39
Stress, 85, 98, 101-102, 105
Study Charts, 7, 9, 10, 45, 91
Subjects, 7-10, 12-13, 15, 17-20, 22, 25-26, 28, 35-36, 41-43, 45, 47-48, 53-59, 68-69, 72-77, 79-81, 102, 106, 110, 121
Summer, 2-3, 52-53, 102, 112, 120, 122
Supplementing, 17, 18, 20, 23, 26
Supplies, 5, 15, 20-21, 23, 26-31, 33-36, 39, 48, 55, 61, 63, 68, 70, 81, 91-93, 95, 111
Support Group, 2-3, 6, 27, 29, 71, 99, 103, 106-109, 114
Tattletales, 95
Teachable Moment, 56, 59, 67
Teacher's Manuals, 15, 19, 26, 52, 74
Teaching Methods, 12-14
Teenager, 23, 54, 60, 74-78, 80-81, 100-101, 104, 105, 108-109, 111, 113, 114
Television, 5, 8, 17, 19, 46, 58, 64, 70, 82, 85, 89, 97, 103
Testing, 3, 22, 73, 76
Tests, 3, 22, 73, 76
Textbooks, 13, 29, 93
Time Management, 45, 46, 53-55, 83, 105
Toddlers, 61-64, 71, 111, 113, 120, 123
Tomato Staking, 97, 121
To-do List, 10, 45, 47, 57
Toys, 46, 59-64, 68, 84, 95-96, 114

Transcript, 10, 13, 75-76
Transitioning to Homeschooling, 4
Traveling, 77, 101
Trivium, 12
Tutor, 74-75
Tutorials, 30, 75
Umbrella Schools, 18, 22, 75, 102, 112
Unit Studies, 13, 25
Unschool, 7, 10, 13, 56, 66, 119
Used Books, 28, 30, 36, 108
Used Curriculum, 25, 26, 27, 29, 30, 35,
    36
Vacations, 53, 101-102
Video Courses, 13, 74
Videos, 8, 13, 17-18, 20, 27-28, 60, 64,
    74, 82
Virtual Field Trips, 20-21, 27-28, 39, 65,
    92
Volunteer Work, 8, 76-77, 101, 114
Web Sites, 4, 13, 16-17, 19, 21-22, 26,
    28, 32, 50, 73, 81, 109
Whining, 85, 96-97
Wife, see Spouse
"Witching" Hour, 95
Work-at-Home, 81
Workbooks, 9, 13-15, 17-20, 23, 25, 28,
    35, 38-39, 46, 59, 63, 68, 80, 89
Workshops, 19, 105
Working Parents, 79, 81-82
Year-round Homeschooling, 52, 80, 101-
    102

0-595-34259-0